Garden Plants *for* Central Otago

Garden Plants
for Central Otago

Ralph Markby

Longacre Press

To my son Geof,
who encouraged me to write this manual,
and to my wife Judith,
whose comments on the text and selection
of colour plates have been invaluable.

I'm grateful also to Dr Peter Johnson
for his assistance with botanical names
and associated details.

Front cover landscape photograph is by Peter Johnson. All the other cover and text photographs are by the author. Some photographs have been previously published in the Dunedin Rhododendron Group 'Bulletin' and are reproduced here by kind permission of the Dunedin Rhododendron Group.

ISBN 1 877361 16 X

First published by Longacre Press, 2005
30 Moray Place, Dunedin, New Zealand

A catalogue record for this book is available from
the National Library of New Zealand.

Book design by IslandBridge
Cover design by Christine Buess
Printed by Everbest Printing Company, China

Contents

Preface   7

Central Otago and the Lakes District   9

An introduction to garden development   18

Plant lists   35

  ■ Trees for the smaller property   36

  ■ Trees for larger areas   55

  ■ Conifers   60

  ■ Shrubs   70

  ■ Perennials   106

  ■ Ground cover   144

  ■ Climbers   146

  ■ Rock gardens   151

References   163

Plant sources   164

Index   165

Preface

In this book, I am taking the bold step of giving advice to others about what trees, shrubs and perennials may be grown successfully in Central Otago and the Lakes District. My practical experience has been gained in the Wanaka district over the past 30 years while knowledge of the rest of the region has of necessity been restricted to visiting gardens and talking to their owners. I believe, however, that the climatic and soil variations throughout the region do not preclude plants from one area being grown successfully in another. Conditions for growing in the Wakatipu basin are probably the most benign, while by comparison the Cromwell and Alexandra districts have much less rainfall and more sandy and gravelly soils than elsewhere. Summer and winter temperatures do not vary dramatically throughout.

Ownership of a piece of land usually triggers some sort of interest in the soil, even if it is only to sow a lawn. Of course a lawn is usually followed by something else, a border or two and perhaps some shrubs and trees. This was the pattern I followed in my mid-thirties but I was lucky to be living close to the Dunedin Botanic Gardens. It was in the Rhododendron Dell where I was first attracted to these flowering shrubs and I subsequently became enamoured of them. From this start in horticulture it was easy to move on to other plants such as alpines and perennials and finally trees. Trees, of course, *should* come at the beginning as they are the basic structure of any worthwhile garden before planting takes place.

My forty years of working with plants as an amateur horticulturist have taken me beyond the confines of domestic gardens into such places as the woodland garden at Tannock Glen in Dunedin where I spent 18 years of my spare time, on to golf courses for tree planting programmes both in Dunedin and Wanaka, highway tree planting in our district and so on. It has been fascinating working in two distinct areas where the climates are so different.

In Central Otago and the Lakes District the climate is unique in New Zealand and this is partly what prompted me to write about those plants which are most likely to grow here.

What contributes most to the making of an horticulturist are curiosity, observation and a willingness to read some of the many good books available. We have some widely differing characteristics in our region which do need to be observed and studied in order to get the best results. Despite the climatic extremes there are rewards for those who take the trouble to follow this philosophy. I hope what follows will be of some help to those who live in and enjoy this fascinating part of New Zealand.

Ralph Markby, March 2005

Central Otago and the Lakes District

The purpose of this book is to identify and list those plants which find our regional climate to their liking. Many can be grown satisfactorily in both coastal and inland climates but there is a group of plants which do well in the softer climate of the east coast, Dunedin in particular, but which will not be hardy enough for Central Otago and the Lakes District. Conversely many plants which thrive in this area will not tolerate the damp, poor drainage and lesser sunlight of the coast. I have endeavoured to compile a list of trees and shrubs which should grow happily and survive long term.

A distinction has been made between smaller trees which can be accommodated on a section of land up to 1000 sq metres (one quarter acre) and those larger and often more dramatic trees which can be sited more easily on a larger property. Development of land for building sites has moved at an extraordinary rate in recent years bringing with it a need to consider carefully what trees and shrubs to plant on a small site. Problems with neighbours crop up when this requirement is not observed and one of the factors which prompted me to tackle this project was the need to catalogue the many smaller trees which are available. Too often on a small site one sees unsuitably large trees which have been gruesomely topped to control growth. Unfortunately vigorous trees like Silver Birch, Elm and others make quick secondary growth so that within a year they are back to their earlier height with several growth leaders where previously there was one. The effect remains ugly and unsightly in a different way.

For the past 15 years, I have gardened more intensively and have had to learn how to cope with the vagaries of climate and soil. How to sow lawns, set up irrigation systems, select suitable shrubs and trees for wind shelter, learn how tall trees grow before buying, create an area of micro-climate within the garden if the natural land forms do not provide this, learn to make compost from what is locally available, find out about frost hardiness of some plants, learn about our native species and discover that some of them can be difficult to grow.

Climate statistics

Before dealing with these garden problems, I would like to say something about the four towns or regions in this survey. Climate statistics reveal some interesting facts. Firstly, rainfall, a vital element in horticulture differs widely. The following table gives a comparison:

Average annual rainfall 1982–2002	
Alexandra – the driest town in New Zealand	334 mm
Cromwell with not a lot more rainfall comes next	446 mm
Queenstown and the Wakatipu Basin owe their verdant landscape to the moister climate	789 mm
Wanaka is close to the Main Divide and benefits accordingly	650 mm

It is clear that supplementary watering is required throughout the region, particularly in Alexandra and Cromwell. Wanaka has its own problem, being possibly the windiest area. Drying winds for two or three months through spring and summer dehydrate the soil and even a night's downpour can be sucked dry within 48 hours by strong northerly winds. Fortunately all four towns have an assured water supply through proximity to the Clutha River or Lakes Wakatipu and Wanaka.

Average temperatures

As regards temperature, there is less difference among the four regions than might be supposed and surprisingly it is Cromwell which has the highest average maximum temperature over an admittedly longer period of review.

The author's garden in winter, August 2004.

	Average extreme maximum air temperature (°C)	Average extreme minimum air temperature (°C)
Alexandra (1992–2003)	31.7	− 7.7
Cromwell (1984–2003)	32.3	− 7.6
Queenstown (1991–2002)	29.1	− 6.8
Wanaka (1992–2003)	30.9	− 6.2

The average extreme heat and cold temperature figures have been used as these temperatures can cause the most problems to plant life and limiting which plants can be grown. Otherwise temperatures are reasonably temperate throughout.

Soil conditions

Having dealt with rainfall and temperature, the last key element affecting horticulture is soil. It goes without saying that sunshine hours are more than adequate.

The Wakatipu basin is the most favoured, with good quality loamy silt and sandy loam extending to considerable depth. Water retention of these soils is above average for the region.

Around the shore of Roy's Bay at Wanaka is a shallow margin where gravels are close to the surface with only a thin layer of loamy sand cover. Elsewhere within the greater town boundaries are considerable areas of sandy loam.

Cromwell soils are formed on dune sand but have been developed, to give good growing conditions. The Cromwell and Bannockburn district has proved to be excellent for horticulture such as stone fruits and grapes.

Alexandra's terrace consists of gravelly loamy sand with better country on the Earnscleugh flats. Despite the unpromising appearance of some of these soils they have proved productive both commercially and domestically.

All the soils of the region lack structure and deficiencies of magnesium, iron and trace elements may occur. To produce good growing conditions for garden plants and help water retention, the addition of organic compost is very desirable. The climate we enjoy in this region is as close to a continental one as is found in New Zealand. It has the advantage of well defined seasons so that plants usually know what to expect, especially those which come from North America, Europe and Asian countries such as China and Japan. It is a region free of the very sudden and substantial temperature changes of the east coast. Rainfall may occur infrequently with longish dry spells. There are pluses and minuses in our climate and soils but overall we have a favourable environment for many good trees and shrubs.

Some favourite plants

When I lived in Dunedin, for many years, rhododendrons were one of my favourite plants and I was able to grow all the tender species which are generally very beautiful both in flower and foliage. In Wanaka, the same plants were a failure. Flower buds were regularly frosted and planting under conifers or the use of frost cloth were to no avail. Two other favourites were also marginal.

I know that magnolias are grown quite extensively in parts of the region but my experience was to find late frosts burnt off the new leaves from which there was no recovery. I did succeed however with *M. salicifolia*, a very beautiful white flowered magnolia which can give the appearance of cherry blossom when in full flower. I have seen *M. soulangeana* and *M. stellata* doing well here so I believe some sites and some species will succeed while others will not. There does not seem to be any simple rule.

Likewise the Japanese maples (*Acer palmatum* species and cultivars) are sometimes prone to have their new foliage destroyed by late frosts. They also suffer die-back of the woody extremities if exposed to wind. Only the Japanese maples are affected in this way, all the others being very hardy. Where these marginally hardy plants are concerned it seems that one has to experiment and take the odd risk. Frost pockets in low lying ground with no air drainage are places to avoid for all but hardy plants. Generally speaking however, there is a very good and wide choice of things to plant, many of which would not do as well or survive at all in coastal gardens. Our great advantages are our free draining soil and long sunshine hours – a priority for the great majority of plants. One exception I can think of is the Asiatic primulas of which there are a great number. In the soil of our garden in Dunedin they thrived because the roots were always moist and they could penetrate the heavy soil. But there are not many plant families with this preference.

Rhododendrons do well enough but they should be protected from sun and wind, as they should be anywhere. Partial shade afforded by larger trees is best. It also pays to grow the hardier hybrids or ones which flower late October and November to avoid late frost damage to blooms. These also withstand dry conditions better. Some of the highly desirable *Rhododendron* species do very well in our garden – two particular groups, the *pogonanthum* and *campylogynum* species. Terrible names to conjure with.

The first group comes from Kashmir and likes our light free draining soil. They will not grow on the coast. They have small daphne-like flowers of pink, lemon and white and have been used to produce some very nice hardy dwarf hybrids.

The *campylogynum* rhododendrons have small thimble shaped flowers of plum colours to salmon above very attractive shiny foliage. They are also dwarf plants.

R. augustinii is a beautiful hardy species, which I grow. Its lavender blue flowers come closer to a true blue than most other rhododendrons.

Azaleas (part of the genus *Rhododendron*) don't mind more sun than rhododendrons and do well.

Camellias are very hardy plants and they thrive, provided they are planted on a south or east facing wall or equivalent shelter as both the foliage and flowers need protection from the sun.

Paeonies are particularly successful as they enjoy reasonable exposure to the sun.

Roses likewise are sun lovers and do well here but require more attention than most plants – feeding, spraying and pruning. The dedicated rose-lover will always grow them despite the work but when not in flower they are not as attractive as many other leafy shrubs. As single plants they can be merged in with other plants successfully or they can be arranged in a formal rose garden where they probably look their best. They are also extremely effective as climbers.

Cornus is a genus of hardy small trees, and very popular. The species mentioned in the list of plants are widely grown and put on an unfailing display every spring.

The smokebush, *Cotinus coggygria*, is in a similar category. It makes its claim to fame in autumn when few other trees can compete with its almost incandescent colour. And of course the 'smokes' add interest in summer.

The American oaks have proved to be absolute stalwarts in this region. They can be slow growing but are ultimately large trees suitable for larger properties unless one is prepared to live with them say for ten or fifteen years and cut them down when they outlive their site.

The pin oak (*Quercus palustris*) has beautiful new acid yellow spring growth and equally fine autumn tints of many hues. The scarlet oak (*Quercus coccinea*) has, as its name implies, scarlet autumn foliage with the same attractive spring growth. The red oak (*Quercus rubra*) has much larger leaves, which also colour well.

The oaks put their roots straight down to moisture levels which means they will grow, admittedly more slowly, in quite gravelly country. This makes them easy care in our drier soils. Also they are not troubled by wind which is a great asset. If they have a fault it is a habit of keeping their dead autumn leaves right through winter before shedding them progressively just before the new leaves appear. However this is a small price to pay for their other major qualities. Leaf fall and the tidy up this involves every autumn is a garden chore one must accept in return for the enjoyment deciduous trees provide through spring, summer and autumn. There is always a quid pro quo in living with nature and we have to simply accept this as a fact of life and not expect a one-sided deal from our garden friends. Oak leaves are excellent fodder for the compost bin.

Eucryphia is an evergreen shrub, with admirable foliage and flowers.

E. cordifolia is a medium-sized shrub from Chile, is hardy, wind tolerant, likes our climate and produces beautiful cup-shaped white flowers in late summer. There are various hybrid eucryphias the best known being *E. × nymansensis* (*cordifolia × glutinosa*) which is quick growing, tall and more woody with larger flowers than *E. cordifolia*.

Our native hebes are also invaluable for sunny drier sites. Except for *Hebe macrantha,* the usual white flowers are not spectacular but their rich green (or sometimes grey) foliage is handsome. However one has to beware of over-watering through programmed irrigation. I have lost a few hebes in this way.

The hydrangea is a useful hardy and ornamental shrub which divides roughly into two groups. The common *Hortensias,* or mop headed hydrangea, has many cultivars and they are particularly useful as an everlasting flower for floral decoration. Perhaps the more attractive are the Lacecaps which are daintier in habit. One of the best is 'Blue Wave' which in neutral or acid soils is a good soft lilac to blue. Another Lacecap species is *Hydrangea villosa* which is very attractive both in foliage and flower.

The humble lavender is very useful for line planting against walls, fronting borders or generally filling up an unwanted piece of ground. They do require an annual clipping and tidy up.

A perennial from a very large genus is the penstemon and it gets special mention because of its easy and hardy nature. The earlier spring flowering species and hybrids are smaller and better suited to the rock garden but the larger summer flowering hybrids in shades of pink and white through to red are long flowering and provide colour when there is not much else.

A plant which is currently much in favour is *Trillium* – a North American woodlander which given a cool position does very well in our region and has a very long life. They are not cheap to buy but are a good long-term investment. There are a good number of species, almost all very beautiful small plants.

A long established and traditional favourite is *Viburnum* which is very much at home here. Some are evergreen but most are not. My favourite is *V. plicatum* 'Mariesii' with its lacecap flattened sprays of snow white flowers in spring and fine autumn colour. For delicacy and scented flower, *V. carlesii* is one of the best. All are hardy and don't mind the sun.

The foregoing is a small selection of some of the plants which commonly do well and collectively help to give substantial structure to any garden. When these are in place, the opportunity remains to underplant or fill in with smaller shrublets and perennials of the gardener's choice. This is the process by which good gardens are slowly and patiently put together to form eventually a landscape which should please all who survey it.

An introduction to garden development

Starting from scratch

Faced with developing a raw piece of land there is at least the advantage of a clean piece of paper on which to express ideas. It is both an opportunity and a challenge. Getting it right the first time gives the pleasure of watching growth of lawns, shrubs etc. when bringing those first plans to life. However if too many mistakes are made some of the work may have to be done over again and some years of growth lost in the process. It is important, therefore, to try to get a good result from the outset.

Using a landscape designer

In today's world the number of people who have the time or the inclination to create their own garden environment is diminishing somewhat and landscape architects have an increasing role to play. They have a different approach to the home gardener as their client usually wants a garden which requires minimum care and knowledge to maintain. This automatically changes the nature of plants used and to some extent makes the garden less interesting.

On the other hand, overall effect is being looked for – different shapes, foliage colour and ground cover. It is possible to get a very pleasing picture where a skilful landscaper has been at work and sometimes the client finds an unexpected stirring of interest in a subject which previously was of no interest at all. Of course the landscaper needs to be thoroughly familiar with the garden environment in which he or she is being asked to work, otherwise plants can be sited in unsuitable positions causing their early demise.

Care should be taken in the choice of a landscaper, who should be qualified or belong to an accredited group such as the Landscape Industry Assn of NZ. Also, the client should give the landscaper a brief as to what sort of garden is desired – autumn colour, a native collection, shade trees etc.

The purpose of this book, however, is to help those people who intend doing their own development work and planting, which still applies to the majority of property owners. Even with limited knowledge, great pleasure can be obtained from the creative activity of planting a garden. I hope the comments and advice which follow will be of assistance to this category of readers.

First steps on undeveloped land

There is nothing more daunting than a bare piece of land. Those first steps towards getting something growing are difficult to make and it is desirable to take a leaf from the landscaper's book and prepare a rough scale plan of the land with the house correctly located on it. The next step is to plot the points of the compass so as to envisage the sweep of the sun through the day and from local knowledge the direction of the prevailing wind. In Wanaka, which is more prone to wind than other parts of the region this is of real importance as life without any form of wind protection can be very trying.

Planting a lawn

This is number one priority for most of us and before doing this it is important to have that overall plan of the proposed landscape to ensure the lawn fits into its key role. Generally it is an area from which other parts of the garden may be viewed and accessed and therefore occupies a strategic position. In creating the outer margins of the lawn, a garden hose can be used to give a visual picture. Sweeping curves are preferable to straight lines and a shape which harmonises with the configuration of the land will look more natural.

In our dry climate, getting a lawn established can be difficult. The time of sowing is critical and one is pretty much at the mercy of the weather. The best times of course are in the growth periods of spring and autumn and a warm rain after sowing is a bonus. My limited knowledge of sowing lawns suggests that the soil should be free of lumps and rakeable to give a fine tilth at the surface so that the seed can be raked in and lightly covered. If there is no rain a light watering periodically with a rain sprinkler is best. A sure fire way to get grass seed to germinate is to cover it with pegged down shade cloth. It is worth the cost of using this material, even if the lawn is sown in sections as the germination rate is so good. A generous application of grass seed should be made to counteract a percentage loss in germination, unless the ground is covered with shade cloth when one can expect almost 100 per cent success.

Having got grass to grow, it is then necessary to fertilise it in spring and autumn as there is insufficient nutrient in the soil to support a lawn on an ongoing basis. Using an inexpensive fertiliser dispenser, the work can be carried out quite quickly. Lawn fertilizer is available in 40 kg bags and this is the most economical way to obtain it. If the area of lawn is not too great, an alternative to sowing is to buy in and lay instant lawn which is supplied rolled up in short lengths. It requires skill in laying it, to get a flat surface free of bumps and hollows, but is good for a quick result.

After some years the lawn is likely to build up a 'thatch' below the surface which tends to prevent water reaching the roots and certainly affects the health of the lawn. Contractors can deal with this using a de-thatching machine or they can be hired for personal use.

Shelter from wind

It is normal to work around the boundaries of the property to create the outer framework of the garden and in the process provide some shelter and protection from sun and wind. Summer air temperatures can be quite high and it is desirable from mid-day onward to keep direct sun away from many plants.

When planting trees and shrubs, I use a pole or stake in the ground to represent the tree I am about to plant. Not just one stake but one for each of the proposed planting. When they are all in place it is not too difficult to get a picture of the overall planting and one always finds that stakes have to be moved around quite a lot to get a satisfactory layout. This is much easier than having to shift a tree or shrub after it has been planted when it is obviously in the wrong place. When having placed all the stakes to position the trees, it may be asked how one decides whether the arrangement is right or not. It is a question of trusting the eye. One tends to know instinctively when the picture is right or wrong.

Many factors come into play when doing the initial planting. There are problems here which no amount of advice can solve other than that from someone on the ground at the time. The first and simplest choice is between deciduous and evergreen. It is desirable to have the sun coming through in winter when it is less fierce but not in summer when shade is required and this is a job for suitable deciduous trees. Evergreen trees and conifers are needed more as wind protection and to provide architectural forms which feature all year round.

In a region which is famous for its lake and mountain views, property owners who are favoured in this way will doubtless wish to retain as much view as possible. It is worth noting however that the 'view only' option can be very hard to live with if wind is a factor and there are cases in Wanaka where owners have sold their properties because of it. A compromise which does not at first come to mind is to 'frame' the view between trees which will give some wind protection. In this way the worst effects of wind can be reduced and some view retained. In our first permanent Wanaka property we had a screen of birches which protected us from the prevailing northerly wind but from our dining room we could enjoy through the gaps between the trees good views of Mt Gold, one of the more striking mountains to the north. I know of another case of a friend's house on the lake front at Hawea where earlier planting of larches by the then NZ Electricity Department perfectly framed the view of the lake and mountains at its head. As with a good picture, framing can help rather than detract. Sometimes there is a nearby view of something better unseen and the judicious placing of the right sort of tree can in time deal with this problem.

Another comment I would like to pass on concerns the kiwi obsession with straight lines and neatness – something which must have come from our pioneering and farming heritage. There is a tendency among some of us to 'keep it neat and tidy' and this means lining everything up. In doing this we lose sight of the purpose of planting a garden to embellish the house we live in. That purpose even if it is not consciously recognized is to create a piece of nature around our habitat. And if we give a thought to the way nature goes about it, it is not about regimentation. Trees and shrubs seed themselves around to produce random growth in a perfectly natural way.

It is not easy in a small garden to recreate this effect but with thought and care a more natural landscape can be obtained. The biggest obstacle the garden developer has to overcome is a mental one – that is to get a feel for nature and try and simulate some of its ways. To help this process, small group plantings of trees and shrubs should be made in odd numbers – 1,3,5, and so on. When the numbers are large enough this rule can be discarded.

Getting to know your property

It generally takes at least one year to gain some working knowledge of your land, how it is affected by sun, wind, frost and moisture retention. A close study of what is to be the garden should reveal areas which are hot, cool, dry, moist, sheltered or exposed.

Having done what is possible to minimize the worst effect of these, one is then in a position to consider the choice of plants – what is best suited to the prevailing conditions. A temptation which many of us fall for is to have some special plant we particularly like and try and grow it in a situation it will never survive in. It is so important to choose plants which are most likely to do well in the conditions which exist, after everything has been done to make them as suitable as possible. It is far better to have a healthy plant which you are only moderately fond of instead of an ailing or dead one which you would prefer.

The author's first Wanaka garden.

As this familiarising process develops, first decisions are often modified so that any original landscape ideas are refined as the imagination takes over. If you are a new owner of an existing property it is a good idea to resist wholesale changes in the garden until you have lived with it as it is for twelve months. Some plants which may not have appealed initially may later prove to be quite acceptable. A flexible approach is likely to be rewarding.

Considering your neighbours

On today's small urban sites, it is important when planting trees and shrubs around the boundaries to envisage their effect ten or more years later. For example, the ubiquitous silver birch, an excellent tree in its own right, grows to a considerable height in a short time. This tree seldom survives long without the owner being forced to trim or top it severely, an ugly exercise already mentioned. In addition, it has a root system which will travel any distance in search of water, often into the neighbour's property. The roots are absolute death to a vegetable garden. In this situation it is a tree to be avoided when there are many better alternatives.

Other trees with aggressive root systems are the flowering cherries and some of the maples, the Canadian maple (*Acer rubrum*) being particularly bad. This does not rule them out. It simply makes it difficult to grow anything else close to them. Crabapple (*Malus*) species are excellent in this respect with roots which don't travel. Whatever tree is used it should be sufficiently far from the boundary that it will not unduly overhang the neighbouring property when mature. The most contentious problem is caused by a tree growing up to block or obscure the view from a neighbouring property and is often the cause of bitter argument. By now it will be obvious if peace and harmony are to reign, one should tread warily when planting trees so as to minimize problems in the future.

Planting for healthy growth

Keeping some plants healthy is a challenge but most trees and shrubs can cope easily enough if given water in dry months. They will do even better if some sort of mulch is applied while the ground is moist. Wood chips are useful while 10 cm wads of pea straw are better as they eventually rot down into good compost. Pea straw is better kept away from the front of the border as birds cause havoc in the spring scattering it far and wide. If birds are causing trouble such as excavating the front of borders or undermining plants, I have found that erecting a vertical barrier of 15 cm wide black plastic netting such as that used to cover spouting, is an effective deterrent. It is not conspicuous.

A top dressing of compost is beneficial for rhododendrons, azaleas and many perennials. In this region, the use of sawdust in compost is better avoided, as it holds no moisture and in fact repels water simply making dry soil even more difficult to irrigate. It is quite the reverse in coastal areas where a damper climate and more regular rainfall keeps it moist until it finally rots down.

Yellowing or chlorosis of the foliage of rhododendrons and camellias can occur possibly due to magnesium or iron deficiency or both. Trace elements can also help correct this. The leaves of camellias will often appear bleached and yellow but this is more often caused by too much sun. They prefer a shady situation well away from the sun. In the Lakes District there are often pockets of more acid peaty soil which particularly suits rhododendrons and camellias. Neutral pH soil is more common and the above treatment is quite often needed.

Where mulching is employed the usual chores of weeding and forking over the soil for aeration can be greatly reduced making a huge saving in garden maintenance. Summer weeding is the greatest bugbear for the serious gardener. It is something which must be done otherwise weeds such as cress, clover and others can take root in the heart of valued plants creating a very difficult job of removing them. Sometimes the whole plant has to be dug up in order to remove the offender. And finally the most essential element to ensure growth is water at the right time. An irrigation system of some sort is a must and this will be dealt with separately.

Black Peak 2283 m, Matukituki Valley. Telephoto from the author's home.

Micro climates

This term is used to describe the identifying or creation of special areas within a garden where plants can enjoy something akin to their natural environment. For example if dealing with shade loving plants which need a cool and moist root run such as Asiatic gentians it is no use exposing them to full sun as they will be dead within a year. The challenge is to find or create a shady area where preferably the ground is sloping towards the south or east. Failing this, planting behind a north or west facing wall can help.

Planting under the right sort of trees will also help particularly if there is some shrubbery up to a metre or so on the north or west side. I have found the Japanese crabapple (*Malus floribunda*) a good shade tree once it has put on some growth and some pruning has been done as will be mentioned later. Its roots cause no problem and it is also a very fine blossom tree in the spring.

Pruning

There are some gardeners who consider pruning as something which must be carried out regularly as part of gardening. Up to a point this is correct but when it becomes a ritual 'hair cut' applied to everything in the garden just to stop the plants getting above themselves, then the point has been lost. The plants suffer physically and the landscape effect is spoilt. The theory goes that plants need to be pruned and it is good for them. In practice, many plants don't need to be pruned at all and some suffer because of it. Firstly, there are some small trees and shrubs which do benefit from pruning. Some of the crabapples are notorious for growing in all directions with branches often changing direction at acute and ugly angles. One of the best, the Japanese crabapple (*Malus floribunda*), requires regular pruning to encourage upward growth and this has to be carried out for some years before it gets the message. Another popular small tree, the smokebush (*Cotinus coggygria*), makes long woody new growth which simply has to be cut back hard to the nearest bud. It comes away again quite quickly. The rule should be that any shrub which makes this type of rapid and unruly growth which spoils its symmetry should be carefully pruned.

Popular shrubs such as rhododendrons and camellias do not require pruning at all. Conifers lend themselves quite readily to clipping and can of course be made into formal subjects in this way.

Another type of pruning, which I believe should always be carried out, is on younger trees that may branch from almost ground level. It is generally recognized that the lower part of the trunk should be bare so as to retain a sense of proportion. This is best done progressively as the tree grows, so that ultimately there might be a metre or more of bare trunk. Keep in mind that bare trunks can often be attractive as in the case of some of the white barked birches. It is important to remove these lower branches when they are small in diameter otherwise the scars will disfigure the trunk.

The flowering cherries should be pruned with care as large open cuts can attract disease. An old rule was to cut nothing thicker than your finger. In our drier district I think they are less at risk but it is a good idea to use a pruning paste to cover the cut and help the healing process. A large cut on any tree should be so dealt with. I also remove unwanted branches as close as possible to the trunk to avoid unsightly 'coathangers'. I believe there is some debate among arborists about these procedures but I have never seen any ill effects.

There is a positive side to pruning when done by an expert. Many trees and shrubs can be improved in appearance by the skilled and judicious removal of seemingly unimportant twigs and small branches. The acid test is if, after pruning, the tree doesn't look as if it has been touched at all but somehow looks more attractive, then the operation has been successful. Generally, pruning should be used judiciously to improve the appearance of a tree or shrub and then only when it is obviously needed. Sadly and too often, it produces the reverse effect of plant abuse.

Irrigation

There is no part of the region where irrigation in some form will not be necessary. The Wakatipu basin is probably the moistest area being a natural catchment surrounded by hills but it too can go without rain for long periods. Manual watering is possible but it requires a lot of time moving sprinklers around. The best device for larger areas is the oscillating rain sprinkler which simulates natural rain better than any other. The two hour clockwork water timers makes manual watering more practical as it is just a matter of setting and forgetting. Otherwise it is too easy to forget to turn off the tap. These timers are reliable and inexpensive and if there are enough outside taps available, hoses can be scattered around the property together with appropriate sprinklers so that lawns and garden can be watered progressively. This sort of watering system is the cheapest to set up and will provide a reasonable safeguard against dry periods.

The next stage is still a do-it-yourself operation but one which leaves all the sprinkler system permanently in place. In our previous large Wanaka garden I used micro jets on 30 cm stands screwed into lengths of 19 mm black plastic irrigation pipe. With a supply of the right fittings and tube it was possible to get complete coverage of all the garden borders, banks etc. with clockwork timers fitted to the various taps. To maintain water pressure it was necessary to water in stages but when it is simply a matter of setting the timers, it is a practical system. The one problem with micro jets is that they get blocked from time to time necessitating removal and clearing with a fine piece of sharpened wire. I found that two hours of watering with micro jet sprinklers did allow reasonable saturation of the upper layer of soil and when done regularly kept plants healthy.

The most expensive solution is to call in an irrigation specialist. They plan a simple network of underground plastic pipes, electric solenoid valves and pop up sprinkler heads capable of watering over a radius of 5 m and more. Tall permanent upstands are used to give coverage of taller plants. They also use micro jets on narrow borders and sometimes small adjustable dripper nozzles in confined areas.

Our present property is equipped with programmed irrigation where the watering is carried out through 12 separate stations to maintain adequate water pressure in each. It is all computer controlled with the number of minutes of watering at each station adjustable at will as are the days when watering takes place. Its main purpose is to save time and labour which it undoubtedly does. However, nothing is perfect and I have lost a number of hebes through over watering. Had I reduced watering times, other plants would have suffered. So in the end we sometimes find ourselves using manual sprinklers to concentrate watering in a particular area which needs more. Even with automatic irrigation I find that judicious use of the rain sprinkler on the rock garden is very beneficial.

One has to remember that irrigation is only a substitute and it can never be comparable to a good soaking from 25 mm of rain. It is important not to regularly overwater as natural rainfall does not occur in this way. Leaching of the soil can result. We also have to be mindful that although our water sources are unlimited, storage is not and Council rumblings about water metres send a chilling message to the serious gardener. For property owners who only use their houses for holidays, watering with programmed irrigation is more of a problem as there are times of heavy rainfall when this is counter-productive. I suppose too much is better than none at all but watering on a modest scale would be preferable.

Compost – a valuable ally

Every property produces a quantity of green waste which can be profitably turned into compost and, as already mentioned, our soils cry out for feeding. I don't pretend to know too much about compost making as for many years my wife enthusiastically carried out this process. Out of sheer necessity and a guilty conscience I have recently become more and more interested in compost production. In earlier years, we used very large quantities of rotted pine needles as mulch for the rhododendrons and associated plants. These were eventually absorbed into the soil and, despite the suggestion by some that they exude a toxic substance, we found that our shrubs and smaller plants always showed real signs of benefit. Many sources of this material have disappeared so we now place almost total reliance on green waste. Cow manure, if it can be obtained, makes an excellent constituent but sheep manure, which is often available, can bring in weed such as clover and stinging nettle.

We have long used bins for the rotting down process, unit sections of which are added when more capacity is needed. When each square frame is added it leaves an air space of approximately 6 cm. The timber is tanalised pinus and the bin material can still be bought from a sawmill in unassembled form. The frames are about 1 m square and 15 cm deep. We stockpile our grass clippings and layer them with green waste from the kitchen. Blood and bone meal is also added to the layers and the whole mix is turned periodically. It is not allowed to dry out. In the autumn many gardeners will have the tiresome chore of collecting the leaf fall and these too can be stockpiled for use in the layering process. Many people use leaf vacuum machines to collect leaves and some of these can be had with a mulching attachment which chomps up the leaves as they are collected, making them quicker and easier to compost.

Composting in this way is not a fast process and can take six to nine months but a cubic metre of the finished result will make a lot of plants happy. It should be applied as mulch to a depth of say five cm particularly over the plant's root system and allowed to become part of the soil. If left alone by the birds it will also greatly reduce weed growth.

Native trees and shrubs

Our native flora may not be as colourful as that of other countries but many of our natives make up for this in form and foliage character. At present there is a trend to use native plants anywhere and everywhere as a display of national pride. This is all very well but one has to go back to the golden rule that you plant only what will survive and prosper. One day when we were planting trees beside the highway close to Wanaka I was accosted by a young man who was deeply critical of us for planting exotic trees and not natives. I had difficulty in explaining that firstly, there was no native tree which would grow large enough or survive well in this situation and, secondly, avenue planting demanded deciduous trees with height, form and autumn colour.

In our fairly dry region only some natives enjoy the climate. Kowhai, for example, look wonderful at Glendhu Bay with its generous rainfall whereas in the town they can look stunted without artificial watering. The following is a selection of native plants which I think should prove reliable in most parts of the region. I can understand people becoming very fond of our native flora as it has a character all of its own and will stand comparison with plants from many other parts of the world.

Astelias have recently become noticed due perhaps to their use by landscapers in public areas where they have proved colourful and ornamental. They have silvery green spear like leaves, are quite slow growing but ultimately may reach one metre. They can have a place in the ornamental garden.

Our native beeches (*Nothofagus*) are pretty much confined to the mountains and outliers of the main divide where they receive ample rainfall. They are not really suited to smaller properties and are liked more for their rugged character than for showy effect. They look very natural when in a streamside or water location which is sometimes possible in public areas such as Bullock Creek in Wanaka.

The ubiquitous *Hebe* enjoys drier conditions and some will not tolerate wet feet. There is a wide choice of plants with variable size and foliage. One of my favourites is *H. hulkeana* or New Zealand lilac which given the right site will become usefully rampant. The whipcord hebes are very attractive. They have either bronze or rich green foliage. *Hebe pinguifolia* cultivars have blue grey foliage sometimes edged with red and are very distinctive. Their moisture requirements vary and trial and error is needed to resolve this. There are also some good dwarf species such as *H. buchananii* and a larger-growing *H. macrantha* which has the largest flower of the genus.

Helichrysums are unusual small plants, good for a small garden or space. *H. coralloides* has yellow daisy flowers on grey foliage. *H. selago* is more of a small shrublet to 30 cm with very attractive whipcord growth.

The manukas (*Leptospermum*) are happy anywhere and are very likeable shrubs or small trees both in foliage and flower. There has been a lot of hybridizing to vary the size and colour of the flowers (deep crimson to various shades of pink and white). Some still get affected (but not fatally) by the manuka blight but I suspect those with some Kanuka (*Kunzea ericoides*) parentage are likely to be more blight free. Most will tolerate wind, frosts and varying moisture levels, particularly if they have come from a hardy plant nursery.

The Marlborough rock daisy (*Pachystegia insignis*) is an excellent small shrub which has done well in all our Wanaka gardens and should be happy anywhere in the region. It has large white daisy flowers and striking foliage of quite large deep green felted leaves.

Pittosporums are extremely useful small trees, good for shelter and wind resistance. Several species and some cultivars are growing in our region but the lemonwood (*Pittosporum eugenioides*) is not always hardy. We lost a nine-year-old specimen after a long winter of hard frosts and wind. A nearby hedge of pittosporum also had a number of gaps after three years. *P. tenuifolium* is much hardier but less attractive although *P. tenuifolium* 'Stephens Island' is quite handsome and seems to be hardy. There are a large number of smaller growing variants of this pittosporum varying in height from 1 to 2 m.

Tussock grasses (e.g. species of *Chionochloa and Poa*) are very popular at time of writing and on a patch of otherwise neglected land they make a very pleasing sight. However they look anything but right when mixed with exotic plants. I have seen one bizarre example of a large-scale planting of rhododendrons interplanted with tussocks. Oh dear! Keeping them weed free until they cover the ground is a problem but mulching with wood chips can help.

A word about perennials

The name perennial embraces a vast array of plants from tiny alpines to larger herbaceous species. A loose definition means 'long living', although in practice length of life may depend on factors outside the plant's control such as basic growing conditions. By comparison 'annuals' are plants which die after they flower relying on germination of self-sown seed to survive another year. Some are so successful at this that they can become a weed. Many perennials die down in late summer, often disappearing completely until spring, making it necessary to mark their position in the garden. Some of the smaller woody plants included in the perennial section may be regarded botanically as shrubs but because they are often small or prostrate and used in with small herbaceous plants I have put them in this section.

A few of the herbaceous plants which are frequently seen here would include *Anemone*, *Alstroemeria*, *Aquilegia*, *Astilbe*, *Campanula*, *Chrysanthemum*, *Dianthus*, *Epimedium*, *Gentiana*, *Geranium*, *Helleborus*, *Iris*, *Paeonia*, *Penstemon*, *Phlox*, *Pulsatilla*, *Primula* and *Ranunculus*. Together with the dwarf or smaller shrubs they colonise rock gardens, borders, spaces between shrubs and other areas of prominence.

Some offer useful ground cover such as *Arctostaphyllos nevaedensis*, *Dryas octopetala* and *Tiarella cordifolia*. In the plant list which follows there is a representative selection without getting into the realms of collectors' plants of which there are many. Collectors' plants create great interest through their beauty and rarity, the challenge to grow them and the satisfaction if one is successful but this is outside the scope of this book.

The landscape

Few of us are insensitive to a beautiful landscape as we are fortunate enough to live in a region which is blessed with endless natural beauty. So we are primed to some degree to be able to cast a critical eye on our own creative achievements. In this case, we are talking about gardens where most of us are constrained by our boundary fences and nearby houses. If one is clever enough to meet this challenge by creating a sense of shelter, seclusion and privacy and at the same time intensively plant a lot of interesting small plants, then this is a garden to savour.

I have seen such gardens otherwise I wouldn't have thought it possible. They are the result of mental and artistic endeavours and probably give more satisfaction to the owners than would be gained by someone with a much larger estate. I hesitate to give any advice on this subject as the constraints are often complex and difficult. The solution lies in observing the work of others who have been successful and adapting their ideas to your own creations.

Visual learning

Visits to good gardens in your neighbourhood are one of the best ways of obtaining new ideas about plants and landscaping. In each garden there will be something new or special to trigger an idea for your own. Most gardeners are happy to pass on the name of some admired plant, which may enhance your own collection.

Of course one can't invite oneself into gardens at will but there are generally special occasions when churches, charities and garden clubs invite the public to visit a select list of interesting gardens. There are also gardens where visitors are welcome by appointment.

For those wishing to expand their horizons, these opportunities should not be missed. Most seasoned gardeners have benefited in this way. I would especially recommend these visits be taken in the spring, when so much is happening in the garden.

PLANT LISTS

Under the various headings that follow, I have listed plants which I'm reasonably sure will succeed in our region. Many of these I have had first hand experience with. I have also tried to ensure that the plants are available from one source or another within the South Island so that if they are not in stock at the nearest garden centre, they should be able to be ordered through them. Botanical names have been used for all plants with the common names (if there are any) as secondary. This is standard practice in the nursery trade as many plants do not have a common name. The lists of plants are not exhaustive.

Although there is a reasonable selection of perennials available from garden centres, the most comprehensive source is from the mail order plant nurseries. Their catalogues give considerable information about each plant, its size, the conditions it likes and so on. One catalogue I receive often contains colour illustrations of the more interesting plants. So, even if the buyer has never heard of the plant before, there is enough information and detail to make the purchase a reasonably safe one and of course because of direct purchasing the cost is attractive.

I greatly value the alpine and perennial plant nurseries, as they offer a comprehensive range of plants as well as some real treasures. Once on their mailing list, one receives catalogues each spring and autumn. And what a pleasure it is sitting back in front of the fire with a fascinating list in front of you, pondering what might suit this or that particular spot in the garden.

Trees for smaller properties

* Deciduous
Conifers are included in the Conifer Section (p. 60)

Acacia – Australian wattle

Alphabetically this genus comes up first and I have included it without wishing to recommend it. It is not overly long lived, it somehow doesn't look at home in our region and the wood is prone to splitting, especially after a snowfall. The seed pods of some of the acacia species create a lot of clean up work.

Acer – Maples*

This genus is a large and very important one, maples being indigenous to many parts of the Northern Hemisphere. They are very ornamental through spring and summer with the autumn colour usually outstanding. With the possible exception of the Japanese maples which can suffer from die-back of their outer extremities, they are hardy. Some have root systems which are aggressive but usually other plants can be grown nearby.

A. capillipes (Japan)
A small tree with striated bark (snakebark) and good leaf colour in spring and autumn.

A. davidii (China)
A small tree with striated green and white bark. Dark green leaves colour well in autumn.

A. davidii 'George Forrest'
More commonly found in cultivation. Excellent autumn colour.

A. griseum – Paperbark maple (China)
A beautiful small tree noted for its peeling bark which reveals cinnamon bark underneath.

Acer davidii 'George Forrest'

Acer japonicum 'Aconitifolium'

A. japonicum 'Aconitifolium' (Japan)
When this tree is available it should be snapped up. Small and slow growing, with outstanding autumn colour.

A. negundo – Box elder (North America)
Medium to large in size with a good head. Useful shade and fairly quick growing.

A. palmatum – Japanese maple
There are large numbers of cultivars of this maple – all attractive and with brilliant autumn colour. Those with red-bronze leaves look good through spring and summer.

A. palmatum dissectum
Many cultivars with leaves divided into five, seven or nine lobes. Shrubby, forming an umbrella shaped plant.

A. palmatum 'Senkaki'
Has red bark which it shows off to great advantage in winter. Its autumn colour is a wonderful splash of apricot and gold.

A. platanoides – Norway maple
Hardy and quite fast growing, borderline in ultimate size but worth considering. The form Crimson King with deep red bronze foliage is very attractive and may not grow as fast as the ordinary form. All very wind-resistant.

A. rubrum – Canadian maple
A beautiful colouring tree which is sold in named forms. A seedling *A. rubrum* will not have the autumn colour of the specially propagated clones. An upright form is *A. rubrum* 'Scanlan', which has beautiful autumn colour. *A. rubrum* 'October Glory' is another cultivar with compact habit and perhaps even better colour.

Aesculus – Chestnuts*

Generally the chestnuts are only suitable for larger properties. However, there is one species which is very suitable for the smaller garden.

Aesculus indica (Indian Chestnut)

A. pavia – Red buckeye (Southern U.S.)
An excellent slow growing small tree with candles of red flowers in spring. It sets and throws seeds with young seedlings appearing from time to time. Worth making an effort to obtain one.

Albizzia julibrissin – 'Rosea'* (Iran / China)

This very distinctive tree with fern-like foliage produces attractive fluffy pink flowers in late summer. It has a good crown and makes an excellent shade tree to sit under.

*Amelanchier canadensis** (North America)

This is a most useful small tree which has a sort of dusky white blossom in spring, more attractive than it sounds and good autumn colour. Very hardy. Only fault is some suckering from the base. These suckers should be removed.

Azara microphylla – Vanilla tree (Chile)

A small evergreen tree with sprays of yellow flowers, vanilla scented. Useful for screening or shelter. There are smaller shrubby species but I'm not sure of their availability.

Cercidiphyllum japonicum (Japan)*

A small to medium-sized tree not much seen in cultivation but which should be. The rounded almost orbicular leaves turn pale yellow to pink in autumn and the habit is quite stately. Well worth having.

Cercis canadensis – Forest pansy (North America)*

A small tree with a broad head and rounded leaves which are a deep coppery colour throughout. Has attractive lavender pea flowers in spring. The ordinary form of the species has green leaves and is less attractive.

> *C. siliquastrum* – Judas tree (Eastern Mediterranean)*
> An attractive small to medium-sized tree with rose lilac flowers in spring.

Cornus – Dogwoods*

Cornus do particularly well in our region and are highly recommended. The white flowers (actually the flower bracts) make a handsome sight and the leaves generally have good autumn colour as well.

> C. 'Eddie's White Wonder' (*C. florida* ×*nuttallii*) is said to be an improvement on *C. nuttallii* and probably is. A superb small tree with flowers 5 cm across. Hardy with good autumn colour.

> *C. florida* (Eastern U.S.) – a small tree, white flowered but quite different to the above. The form *florida rubra* is the one to get or one of its various hybrids which generally have deep rosy flowers reminiscent of an azalea. Modest in size.

> *C. kousa chinensis* (China) A small upright tree, different again from the others both in form and flower. Flowers turn pink quite early. Good autumn colour.

Cornus nuttallii – a popular Dogwood

C. nuttallii (Northwest America) – the one most seen and very similar to 'Eddie's White Wonder'. A first class small tree. Hardy with good autumn colour.

Cotinus coggygria – Smokebush (Southern Europe)*

This large shrub or small tree is extremely popular in our region and deservedly so. Its elliptic leaves are attractive and in autumn they are perhaps the most brilliantly coloured of all autumn foliage. It can make unruly growth which requires pruning back. Hardy and wind-resistant, 'Grace' is a hybrid produced by Hilliers in the UK and has recently proved popular. It has larger leaves than the species with slightly darker and equally glowing autumn colour. Rampant growth a drawback.

Embothrium coccineum – Chilean firebush (South America)

This semi-evergreen tree from Chile makes a striking sight when it produces its orange-scarlet flowers in profusion. Interesting linear-lanceolate leaves. Needs wind protection and a moist site. Inclined to sucker.

Cotinus coggrygia (Smokebush)

Fraxinus – Ash *

From observation in the Wanaka district, the common Ash, *Fraxinus excelsior*, suffers from die-back if exposed to too much wind. This may not happen elsewhere.

> *F. ornus* – Manna ash (Europe, Asia Minor)
> A small tree with an abundance of white frothy flowers in spring. Seems to be unaffected by wind.

> *F. oxycarpa* – Raywood – claret ash (Asia Minor)
> A small to medium tree of compact habit, popular for its deep burgundy autumn colour. Appears to be wind-resistant.

Garrya elliptica (California and Oregon)

A small evergreen tree of stately habit, draped in late winter and early spring with greyish green catkins. Quite spectacular.

Gleditsia triacanthos 'Elegantissima' (Central and Eastern U.S.) *

As its name implies this tree has an elegant form which does not intrude in a smaller garden. It has small-leaved frond-like foliage, is thornless and relatively slow growing.

G. triacanthos 'Sunburst'
A tree with bright yellow foliage, which because of its striking colour may be more difficult to place. Quite often seen here. Thornless.

Griselinia littoralis – Broadleaf (New Zealand)

Renowned in our country as an attractive evergreen small tree, for use as shelter. Not seen that much in our region but should grow in any reasonably moist site. Shiny deep green foliage.

Ilex – Hollies

I. aquifolium – English Holly
This and its various cultivars are all hardy, evergreen and have prickly leaves. The species makes attractive conical specimen trees and the female produces red berries. There are many variations and cultivars, some growing to lesser height with foliage which is variegated in assorted colours and forms.

I. x*altaclerensis* 'Hendersonii'
A non-prickly evergreen holly which grows to 2 m with deep green foliage and brilliant berries.

I. x*altaclerensis* 'Lawsonii'
This evergreen holly has brilliant berries and foliage which has golden centres. 2 m.

There are other hollies which cannot be regarded as hardy for our region except for *I. crenata* which is useful for low hedging.

Kolreuteria paniculata – Golden rain tree (China)*

Another useful small tree with pinnate leaves which turn yellow in autumn. A broad-headed tree of good habit.

Leptospermum – Manuka (New Zealand)

This evergreen shrub or small tree, famous in our country as part of the landscape is a very useful windbreak and in its ornamental forms as a desirable garden plant. There is the vexed question of hardiness however. Hybrids brought down from the North Island may not be hardy here but plants raised in the lower South Island should be. There have been some lovely coloured forms available, some for many years such as *L. scoparium* 'Keatleyi' and *L. scoparaium* 'Martini', pale pink to rose respectively. The downside is these forms of *L. scoparium* are prone to the manuka blight. Recent hybrids which may have involved crossing with kanuka (*Kunzea ericoides*) have been able to shed this weakness. If planting hybrids of uncertain hardiness it is better to plant in spring, giving them the summer to harden off. Don't over-fertilise or water before winter.

For a blight-free windbreak or shelter it is better to plant the kanuka which seems to shrug off manuka blight. I have observed both species on Mt Iron near Wanaka where this is the case. Having tramped the hills in the Dunedin hinterland in my youth and enjoyed the wonderful shelter and warmth which only manuka can provide (as well as firewood for boiling the billy) I am sentimentally attached to this lovable New Zealand species and admire it for its many qualities.

Liquidambar styraciflua – Sweet gum (Eastern U.S.)*

This is a beautiful tree of moderate size which is attractive through spring to autumn when the five- to seven-lobed leaves turn various shades of crimson. It appreciates some shelter and a reasonably moist site.

Magnolia

What magnificent flowering trees these are and worth any amount of effort to grow them. As mentioned previously, they may survive well in one site but not in another, particularly if it is a frost pocket, when the new leaves can be burnt by late frosts. I can only comment on what I have seen growing successfully, bearing in mind I have had some failures.

M. campbellii 'Charles Raffill' (Nepal, Sikkim and Bhutan)*
Of course the great *M. campbellii* with its large pink flowers is the most spectacular of all magnolias but it takes roughly 18 years before it blooms. *Magnolia* 'Charles Raffill' flowers much earlier than this and the flowers are almost as good as its parent. It may be hardy in some areas, and parts of the Wakatipu basin may suit it.

M. grandiflora (Southeastern U.S.)
This wonderful evergreen magnolia is seen quite frequently and is hardy throughout. It is quite unique in appearance with its

Magnolia salicifolia – hardier than other Asiatic species

stiff olive green foliage but when the huge flowers appear in summer it adds another dimension. These flowers are beautifully scented – even from a distance. It has continuous leaf fall creating an ongoing tidy up exercise but is otherwise a great tree for the area.

M. salicifolia – The willow magnolia (Japan)*
This is a magnolia I have had first hand experience with. I found it quite hardy and a rewarding tree to own. The leaves are willow-like (hence the name) and from a distance its white flowers can resemble a flowering cherry. Very worthwhile acquiring.

M. soulangiana (*M. denudata* ×*liliiflora*)*
It has large tulip-shaped white flowers stained rose purple, flowering in October to November. It is a large shrub or small tree with spreading branches.

M. stellata (Japan)*
This is a distinctive, shrubby, slow-growing magnolia reaching little more than 2 m in height. The flowers have strap-like petals and may be blush white or pink. Appears to be quite hardy.

Getting onto more dangerous ground there are a number of beautiful hybrids which may succeed in a sheltered environment not too subject to frost. The Jury family of New Plymouth produced some of these, *M.* 'Vulcan' (deep rose red) being an outstanding example and *M.* 'Iolanthe' another. Slightly more tender species include *M. sieboldii* which has open white fragrant flowers with red stamens. *M. wilsonii* has rather similar flowers which display themselves in pendulous fashion. Either one is worth every effort to grow.

MALUS – Crabapples

There are a large number of cultivars and hybrids of this genus, many of them bearing large fruits which not everybody welcomes. There is a large choice but narrowed down my favourites are:

M. floribunda – Japanese crabapple*

This ultimately modest size tree is great as a shade tree for growing smaller plants beneath as the roots do not intrude. It requires considerable pruning in the earlier years to encourage upward or spreading growth as it tends to shoot downwards. In spring the blossom is outstanding, comparing favourably with some of the cherries.

M. coronaria 'Charlottae Flore Pleno' (Eastern U.S.)*

An excellent smaller tree with large semi-double flowers, pale pink and scented, late November. Leaves colour well in autumn.

M. ioensis 'Plena Bechtels Crab' (Central U.S.)*

It has large semi-double soft pink fragrant flowers 4–5 cm across.

M. 'Profusion'*

Possibly the best of the deep wine red flowering crabapples with colourful young leaf growth. Flowers up to 4 cm across, slightly scented. Fruits small in size. Hardy.

Nyssa sylvatica
(Southern Canada, Eastern U.S. and parts of Mexico)*

This is a beautiful species, not commonly seen but freely available. Should be hardy and its slower growing character makes it ideal for smaller gardens. Would appreciate a site which is not too dry.

N. sylvatica 'Sheffield Park'
Fiery autumn colours. To 3 m.

N. sylvatica 'Vesuvius'
Rich scarlet, orange and yellow autumn colours.

Parrotia persica (Iran to Caucasus)*

A tough and hardy small tree very suitable for the smaller garden. New leaves sometimes have a thin brown edging. Leaves turn to orange and gold in autumn. Fairly slow-growing.

Pistacia

A small group of trees with pinnate leaves, at first sight bearing some resemblance to the rowan.

P. chinensis (China)*

An elegantly shaped small tree with a good crown, which in autumn must be one of the best colouring of all deciduous trees. Available periodically.

Pittosporum (New Zealand)

Some of the *Pittosporum* species are widely used for wind shelter and are popular at present in our region.

P. eugenioides – Lemonwood

This is a reasonably quick growing tree with oblong glossy leaves. It is a little suspect as regards hardiness but in the end there are more successes than failures. It has honey scented pale yellow flowers in spring and there are variegated forms.

P. tenuifolium – Kohuhu

It is reckoned to be hardier than *P. eugenioides* and it too provides good wind protection. There are many cultivars with a range of leaf size, colour and variegation.

P. tenuifolium (Stephens Island)

This form has larger attractive deep green leaves, well displayed on a small tree of pyramidal shape. Hardy in our garden.

Prunus

This is a very large genus which includes many of our best blossom trees, all able to be grown in our region. The genus *Prunus* is distinguished from the apple (*Malus*) and pear (*Pyrus*) by the flowers having a solitary style (that is, the reproductive member which incorporates the ovary at its base and stigma at its tip). I mention this as the feature that links a number of *Prunus* species that might otherwise

Opposite: *Pistacia chinensis* – one of the best autumn foliage trees

appear unrelated, e.g. almond, apricot, bird cherry, Japanese cherries, peach and Portugese laurel.

Prunus armeniaca – Dawn – apricot (Central Asia and China)*
This tree has rich scented blossom in spring with striking effect.

The Cherries*
By far the most widely grown of all the *Prunus* genus, with a large choice from the many Japanese hybrids and cultivars, most of which have their origins well in the past. There are also species and hybrids originating from China and other parts of Asia. Although they will withstand wind they can show their dislike of it, so a sheltered site is preferable. With so much available it is hard to know where to start so I'll begin with an old favourite.

P. 'Accolade'
Semi-double flowers of a clear pink on a sizeable and well-proportioned tree.

P. amanogawa – Poplar cherry (Japan)
A columnar tree with branches erectly held. Clear shell pink semi-double flowers.

P. incisa – Fuji cherry (Japan)
A lovely species, shrubby in shape with fairy-like blossom of blush white but an overall pink effect.

P. sargentii (Japan)
A most beautiful species with handsome bark, single pink flowers and dramatic autumn foliage.

P. shirotae – Mount Fuji cherry (Japan)
Wide-spreading or slightly drooping branches. Double white flowers.

P. subhirtella 'Autumnalis' (Japan)
Produces its semi-double white flowers intermittently through winter and spring. 'Rosea' has blush pink flowers. Great for winter.

P. yedoensis – Yoshino cherry (Japan)

One of the very best cherries. It has exquisite blush flowers which clothe the branches to their tips, creating a wonderful sight. September flowering. There are other cultivars of this species all of which should be good.

Laurel

P. lusitanica – Portugal laurel

An extremely useful, hardy, evergreen shrub or small tree much used for wind shelter and hedging. Good if left to develop as a specimen with attractive white racemes of flowers.

Peach*

P. persica 'Clara Meyer' (China)

Excellent double pink. May be subject to leaf curl necessitating spraying with a fungicide.

Plum*

P. cerasifera 'Nigra' (Balkans, Caucasus, Western Asia)

A small tree with coppery leaves and fragrant white to pink flowers. Hardy and wind-resistant.

P. blireana

A beautiful small tree with leaves metallic copper in colour. Double rose pink flowers, slightly fragrant. Hardy.

Pyracantha – Firethorn (China, Asia Minor and South Europe)

Can be a shrub but some will attain the height of a small tree if allowed to grow unchecked. The thorns are quite fearsome and care must be taken when pruning, something which is usually necessary to keep a reasonable shape. They can also be pruned regularly to create a formal shape. Grown more for their berries which put on a spectacular show.

P. coccinea

A small tree with red berries in clusters.

P. 'Shawnee'
A larger growing tree with yellow to orange berries.

Sophora – Kowhai (New Zealand)

The kowhai is something of a botanical icon among our native plants, probably because of its clusters of brilliant yellow flowers, attractive to bellbirds and other honey-eaters. A handsome tree if well grown.

S. microphylla (South Island kowhai)
Ultimately a small tree with dainty feathery foliage and rich yellow flowers. Dense and twiggy foliage when young.

S. tetraptera (North Island kowhai)
A somewhat larger tree with bigger leaves and denser foliage. Later flowering.

Sorbus Rowan

This is a large and important genus of hardy trees, some of which are very suitable as ornamental trees for the smaller property. There are two sections within the genus, some members of which are commonly grown here. The best known belong to the section Aucuparia, which includes the common rowan, all having pinnate leaves. Trees belonging to the other section Aria have simple leaves quite unlike the former.

S. aria – Whitebeam (Europe)*
A hardy small to medium sized tree with attractive new leaves which are downy grey, white beneath and changing to green later. Russet in autumn with bunches of red berries. Doesn't mind wind.

S. aucuparia – Rowan or mountain ash (Europe)*
A small to medium tree much planted in our region. Good autumn colour and bright red berries much loved by the birds. Most sucker quite badly from the base of the trunk which must be dealt with. There are various improved cultivars available.

Sorbus hupehensis (Chinese rowan) in autumn

S. cashmiriana (Kashmir)*
A beautiful small tree with spectacular white berries which in conjunction with the autumn foliage make a great sight. Highly recommended. Hardy.

S. hupehensis (China)*
A medium size tree with greyish blue-green leaves and pink and white berries in autumn. From a distance the fruits look like salmon pink blossom and added to the autumn foliage colour, it is a wonderful sight.

There are other species and cultivars available but the above are a selection of the most popular.

Stewartia

These small and highly ornamental trees are allied to *Camellia*. The following are the two most commonly found in cultivation here.

S. pseudocamellia (Japan)*
It has white camellia-like flowers with yellow anthers. Flowers are 5–6 cm across, freely produced. Soft subtle autumn foliage colour.

S. sinensis (China)
An elegantly shaped small tree with a good crown. Cup-shaped white flowers 4–5 cm across in the leaf axils. Outstanding autumn colour.

Styrax

There appears to be only one member of this genus of beautiful small trees normally available.

S. japonica (Japan, Korea)*
It has always been available but for some reason it is not much seen in gardens. It has white pendulous bell-shaped flowers better seen from underneath and should be planted with this in mind. A dainty and elegant tree, yet hardy.

Trees for larger areas

* Deciduous
Conifers are included in the Conifer Section

It is quite liberating to be able to write now about trees which can be planted in a freer fashion without worrying too much about them outgrowing the available space or bothering the neighbours. In defining a larger area, I have considered one half acre or 2000 sq m to be a minimum size, just big enough to accommodate a few trees which can be described as large.

On a larger property there is the greater opportunity to create a much better landscape plan and care should be taken in siting trees with this in mind. In the bigger picture, conifers may be considered to provide structure and balance without being allowed to dominate. There is a good number of handsome and desirable specimen conifers which will enhance any landscape if tastefully incorporated with deciduous trees and shrubs. Sun, shade, shelter and view will still have to be taken into account and some skill and knowledge will be needed to create an attractive landscape. If the owner doesn't feel confident in this respect, there is a case for calling in a landscape designer to help.

Aesculus – Chestnuts*

A. indica – Indian horse chestnut (Northwest Himalaya)
A magnificent large tree with pinkish cinnamon coloured new foliage and large panicles of pink flushed flowers.

A. xcarnea 'Briotii' – Red horse chestnut
A hybrid of two species, one large and one small. Compact tree with flowers a deep rose.

Betula – Birches

B. jacquemontii (Western Himalaya)
One of the best of the birches with peeling white bark and ovate serrated leaves which are larger and more attractive than the common birch.

B. papyrifera – Paper birch (North America)*
A large tree, noted for its white papery bark.

B. pendula – Common silver birch (Europe, Asia Minor)
After growing to a considerable height the upper branches become pendulous.

Eucalyptus – Gum Tree (Australia)

The ubiquitous gum tree (evergreen) is seen in many parts of New Zealand but only some species are hardy in our region.

E. gunnii, *E. niphophila*, *E. nicholii* and *E. nitens* are all hardy. *E. nicholii* is attractive as a young plant but less so with age and I have known larger specimens blow over in strong winds.

E. niphophila (Snow gum) has a beautiful trunk mottled pale grey, green and cream and is an attractive specimen tree.

Fagus – Beeches*

F. sylvatica – Common beech (Europe)
The so called Englishbeech is a large spreading tree of noble proportions and excellent autumn colour

F. sylvatica 'Riversii' – Copper or purple beech
A magnificent large specimen tree with outstanding deep colour.

Juglans – Walnut (Southeast Europe, Himalaya and China)*

J. regia – Common walnut
Ultimately a large tree. For earlier and better quality fruiting, named clones are desirable rather than seedling trees.

Liriodendron tulipifera – Tulip tree (North America)*

A large stately tree. This is the most common of the two species. It has squarish, chunky, four-lobed leaves and greenish flowers marked with yellow and rosy streaks within.

Quercus – Oaks*

Most useful ornamental large trees, most of which do very well in all parts of our region. The American oaks tolerate wind, dry conditions and poor gravelly soils. Most have outstanding autumn colour.

Q. canariensis ×robur

A cross of the Algerian and English oaks. Quick growing, hardy and colourful in autumn.

Q. coccinea – Scarlet oak (Canada, U.S.)

Glowing scarlet in autumn. Hardy and wind-resistant.

Q. palustris – Pin oak (Canada, U.S.)

Many-hued autumn colours, hardy and wind-resistant. Will grow in most situations. An outstanding tree for our region.

Q. robur – English oak (Europe, Caucasus, Asia Minor, North Africa)

Slow growing and less showy than the American oaks. More of a park tree for more sheltered sites.

Q. rubra – Red oak (Eastern U.S.)

Larger fleshier leaves than the other oaks. Deep red autumn colour. They all tend to retain their dead autumn leaves until the following spring.

Robinia pseudacacia – False acacia (Eastern U.S.)*

A large, hardy and quick growing tree.

Salix babylonica – Weeping willow (China)*

A hallmark shade tree for Central Otago and the Lakes District. Nothing better if sufficient space and the right site can be found. Quite fast growing.

Tilia – Lime or linden tree (Europe, Asia, North America)*

T. xeuropea – Common lime

A cross of several species, it has been much used in the past for avenue and street planting. A large tree in time with sweetly scented flowers in January.

T. mongolica (North China)

A smaller tree of compact rounded habit.

T. platyphyllos (Europe)

Vigorous tree of rounded habit. A good specimen tree.

Ulmus – Elm*

U. procera Louis van Houtte – Golden elm

A popular specimen tree with leaves which are part green and bright golden throughout summer.

Zelkova – Allied to the elm*

Z. serrata (Japan, Korea, China)

A large spreading tree of graceful habit and good autumn colour.

Opposite: *Quercus palustris* (Pin oak) – a stalwart of the region

Conifers (Cone-bearing trees)

Conifers vary in size tremendously which means there is a choice from tiny to small rock garden specimens to very large trees. At present they appear to be out of fashion for urban gardens but it is a mistake to exclude them totally from any garden. Their main virtue is that they provide year-round form, colour and texture when some of our more glamorous shrubs and trees are exhibiting nothing better than winter's bare wood. For this reason they make for good balance in the garden provided they are not over-planted. Good landscaping rules still apply. With one or two exceptions they are all evergreen.

Dwarf conifers – Evergreen

These are desirable evergreen shrubs for rock gardens, small borders or open spaces. Properly placed, they can complement the perennials.

Abies – Fir

A. balsamea 'Nana' – Dwarf balsam fir
Dark green, compact foliage, handsome new growths 30 cm.

Chamaecyparis – False cypresses

C. lawsoniana 'Green Globe' 30 cm.

C. obtusa 'Kosteri'
Deep green foliage, bronze in winter. 50 cm.

C. obtusa 'Nana Gracilis'
Handsome foliage in attractive whorls. 75 cm.

C. pisifera 'Filifera Nana'
Thread-like green foliage. 75 cm.

Abies balsamea 'Hudsonia' – a popular dwarf conifer

Cryptomeria – Japanese Cedar

C. japonica 'Vilmoriniana'
Green in summer, bronze in winter, fine feathery foliage. 50 cm.

Juniperus – Junipers (good ground cover)

J. communis 'Hornibrookii'
Blue-green foliage, flat ground cover. 25 cm.

J. squamata 'Blue Star'
Silver-blue foliage, slow growing. 30 cm.

J. xmedia 'Gold Coast'
Gold prostrate juniper. 40 cm.

Picea – Spruce

P. glauca 'Conica'
Conical slow growing, rich green. 1 m.

Thuja

T. occidentalis 'Caespitosa'
Summer green, winter bronze. 40 cm.

T. orientalis 'Blackman's Blue'
Blue green in summer to winter bronze. 1 m.

Thujopsis

T. dolobrata 'Nana'
Flattened sprays of foliage turn from green to bronze in winter.
50 cm.

Medium size conifers

Chamaecyparis lawsoniana

'Blue Mountain'
Conical habit, blue foliage. 1.5 m.

'Ellwoodii'
Conical habit, blue green foliage. 1.5 m.

'Grayswood Feather'
Upright green, tidy habit. 3 m.

'Hughes'
Pyramidal shape, silver and blue green foliage. 4 m.

'Imbricata Pendula'
Thin weeping branches of green, elegant specimen. 4 m.

'Pembury Blue'
Upright pyramidal shape, silver blue. 3 m.

'Silver Queen'
Contrasting green foliage with silvery cream tips. 3–4 m.

'Stewartii'
Attractive bright green and gold foliage. 3 m.

Chamaecyparis pisifera (Japan)

'Boulevard'
Dense feathery blue grey. Distinctive colour and form. Quite different from most other conifers.

Cryptomeria – Japanese cedar

C. japonica 'Elegans Compacta'
Soft green foliage changes to bronze in winter. 2 m.

C. japonica 'Elegans Aurea'
Pale green foliage. 2 m.

Cupressus – Cypresses

There are many species in this genus but most are more suited to larger properties. However some of the so called 'pencil' cypresses are useful landscape plants, sited near buildings, gateways and so on.

C. sempervirens 'Gracilis'
Narrow column of bright green. 3 m.

C. sempervirens 'Swanes Gold'
An old favourite with bright golden foliage. 3 m.

C. cashmeriana – Kashmir cypress
A beautiful and graceful tree with weeping, flattened sprays of blue-grey foliage on drooping branchlets. Was freely available a few years ago and should still be around. Succeeds best in a moist site. Moderate size.

Ginkgo biloba

A monotypic genus. Unusually slow-growing and rather beautiful, deciduous conifer of ancient lineage. The fan-shaped leaves turn a striking clear yellow in autumn.

Juniperus – Juniper

J. recurva 'Coxii' – Chinese coffin tree
Slow-growing sage green with graceful drooping branchlets. 3 m.

Picea – Spruce

All species are attractive.

P. pungens 'Koster'
The very popular blue spruce, slow-growing neat pyramidal form.
4 m.

P. smithiana – Weeping Himalayan spruce
Like most weeping conifers, it takes a few years to develop this
habit. Very handsome. 4 m.

Thuja

Not unlike Lawson's cypress but with very aromatic foliage and usually
a conical habit. Will grow in most well-drained soils.

T. koraiensis – Korean thuja
Grey-blue beneath and green on upper side of foliage. 3 m.

T. occidentalis 'Ericoides'
Compact deep green foliage turning to red bronze in winter. 1 m.

T. occidentalis 'Pyramidalis'
Upright grower, green to bronze in winter. 3 m.

T. occidentalis 'Fastigiata'
Narrow columnar habit. 3 m.

T. occidentalis 'Holmstrup'
Upright, dark green foliage. 3 m.

T. occidentalis 'Smaragd'
Formal upright columnar tree, popular in Europe. 3 m.

Opposite: *Cupressus cashmiriana* – beautiful weeping habit

Larger conifers

Abies – Firs

All *Abies* species are handsome stately trees, probably better as single specimens. They tend to be slow-growing hence they are not seen frequently. Plant early in life to enjoy the best of them. Here is a short list:

A. koreana (Korea)
Leaves deep green above, gleaming white beneath. Cylindrical cones violet-purple. 5 m.

A. nordmanniana – Caucasian fir
Leaves shining green above with two white bands beneath. Tiered branches sweep downwards. 5m.

A. pinsapo – Spanish fir
A beautiful conifer of dense conical habit with short tight foliage. Glaucous (blue) form even more attractive. Many good specimens on the Wanaka golf course.

Cedrus

C. atlantica – Atlas cedar (Algeria, Morocco)
Erect stately specimen tree, silvery blue foliage. Reasonably quick growing to 10 m.

C. deodara – Himalayan cedar
A beautiful ultimately large tree of pendant habit. Does well and looks very much at home in the region. Good shelter tree. Slow growing to 10 m.

Cryptomeria – Japanese Cedar

C. japonica
Tall, almost columnar tree with bushy, feathery foliage, pinkish bronze to pale green. Appreciates a moister site. 10 m.

Larix – Larch*

L. decidua – European larch
A handsome tree with drooping branches and good autumn colour. Will not grow easily in dry places and needs to have moisture close by. Deciduous. 10 m.

Metasequoia glyptostroboides – Dawn redwood (China)*

This unusual deciduous conifer was first discovered in China in 1941 and introduced into cultivation in 1947. A shaggy-barked conical tree with flattened leaves becoming pink to old gold in autumn. Tall if well grown and very worth while owning. 10 m.

Picea – Spruce

P. jezoensis var. *hondoensis* – Hondo spruce (Japan)
A medium size, distinctive and unusual spruce.

P. omorika – Serbian spruce
An elegant and beautiful tree, very narrowly conical but ultimately tall, after 25 years or more.

P. orientalis – Oriental spruce (Asia, Caucasus)
Large broadly conical tree with branches to ground level. Highly rated in Europe.

Pinus – Pines

A large genus of evergreen conifers, the best known being *P. radiata*, much used in building construction in New Zealand. Some pine species planted near open country in our region can be a threat as the seeds are so easily spread on the wind. Care must be taken to remove seedlings early on.

P. coulteri – Big cone pine (California, Northern Mexico)
A big tree with very long needles and handsome cones up to 35 cm long. This tree is for the 4 ha. block.

P. patula (Mexico)
A beautiful moderate sized tree with graceful drooping foliage.

Picea omorika (Serbian spruce)

P. sylvestris – Scots pine (U.K., Scandinavia)
A very distinctive and likeable tree of moderate size with sparser blue-green or grey-green foliage and bark faintly mottled orange.

Pseudotsuga menziesii – Douglas fir or Oregon (Western U.S.)

A much-used forestry or shelter belt tree found in many parts of the South Island. Naturalises quickly in the Lakes District. Attractive as a specimen tree and can even be used as hedging. Very easy to establish and ultimately very tall.

Sequoiadendron giganteum – Wellingtonia (California)

One of the oldest living plants in the world. Oldest known age of a felled tree is estimated at about 3200 years. A good number were planted in the early days of settlement in the Lakes District and Central Otago and most still remain as monuments to the past. Tall and conical with downswept branches, it is a tree for the larger estate. Slow-growing in our region.

Thuja plicata – Western red cedar (Western North America)

Large tree with flattened drooping sprays of foliage which give off a pleasant aromatic smell when crushed. Does well in our region. Its timber is imported into New Zealand and much used for better class doors and joinery.

Tsuga heterophylla – Western hemlock (Western North America)

Large, fast-growing tree of elegant shape. Branches drooping and arching. A great tree where space is not a problem.

Shrubs

Shrubs can be broadly defined as woody plants having no trunk, but instead tending to branch from the base. They can vary in size from very small plants of around 20 cm or so, up to 2–3 m tall.

While trees may form the 'backbone' of a garden, shrubs will occupy much of the rest and often form the transition area between the trees, low borders and lawns. The range of shrubs is very wide and I shall be dealing only with the more popular ones, hardy enough for the regional climate.

There are some shrub genera such as *Rhododendron* which within itself contains many hundreds of different species as well as thousands of cultivars. Camellias too, while encompassing a smaller number of species, offer vast numbers of cultivars. Roses are even more diverse. So it is a rich field to explore and one which can be dealt with only in a brief way. Nevertheless this still leaves a very good choice.

Abelia (Asia)

These plants, which grow from 1–2 m, flower in summer and autumn, and enjoy sun.

A. 'Edward Goucher'
Evergreen, bronze new growth with tubular lilac pink flowers. 1.5 m.
A. ×*grandiflora*
Semi-evergreen, with pale pink flowers over a long period 1.5–2 m.

Abutilon

Large shrubs which should be sited against a sunny wall. Noted for producing many lantern-shaped flowers for a long period throughout summer.

Abutilon 'Ashford Red'

A. 'Ashford Red'

I have this tall semi-evergreen shrub growing against a north-facing wall. It produces long-lasting, strawberry red lanterns progressively over three months in summer. A very attractive plant and great value.

A. *vitifolium* (Chile)

Another large handsome shrub requiring a sunny site. Large downy dull green leaves and lilac-blue flowers. Also a white flowered form. There are other hybrids available with typical lantern shaped flowers of yellow and orange.

Azalea

These are now classified within the genus *Rhododendron* and are included with them (see p. 95).

Berberis – Barberries*

Easy to grow in any soil, which is not too wet. Most come from China, other parts of Asia and some from South America. The most readily available are cultivars of *B. thunbergii*.

B. thunbergii 'Atropurpurea'
Foliage rich reddish purple through spring and summer, deepening in winter. Tiny yellow flowers. 1.5 m.

B. thunbergii 'Kobold'
Green foliage in summer turning orange later. 50 cm.

B. thunbergii 'Gold Ring'
Purple leaves edged gold in summer. Good autumn colours. 1.5 m.

Camellia

A very large genus of beautiful evergreen flowering shrubs, the smallest being suitable for a tub and the largest (*C. reticulata*) a small tree. They rival *Rhododendron* for the quality and colour diversity of their flowers although they differ in form and shape. They are not a plant for an open situation as sun bleaches the foliage, particularly the *C. japonica* cultivars. They do best sheltered from sun and wind, especially against a cool wall. There are too many hybrids and cultivars to single out by name – suffice to say that choice (when in flower) is a matter of personal preference. Flowers vary in size from 5 cm to 12.5 cm. They may be single, semi-double, double, paeony form, or formal double (no stamens). I think they look their best as single or semi-double but others may prefer the paeony or formal double forms. Flower colour is predominately pink but there are whites (one with a yellow centre) and true reds. The gradation of colour and form is endless. I would like to mention a few of my own favourites.

C. 'Cornish Snow'
A medium-size hybrid with many small white flowers along the branchlets.

Camellia 'Barbara Clark' – an older, very beautiful hybrid

C. 'Moshio'
Bright red semi-double hose in hose flowers. To 2 m.

C. 'Quintessence'
A miniature Camellia, suitable for a tub. It has scented white, blush pink flowers which appear from mid-winter onwards. Needs frost protection but very worthwhile.

C. reticulata
This is the magnificent 'tree' *Camellia*, quite unlike its bushier relatives. It is expensive and not available everywhere but if one likes beautiful things, this qualifies.

C. reticulata 'Captain Rawes'
This is the original *reticulata* first introduced into cultivation in 1820. It has very large formal double carmine rose pink flowers. There are a dozen or so other cultivars of this species, most of them very desirable and only available from specialist growers.

C. saluenensis (China)

This is one of the small number of *Camellia* species and has been used as a parent for many good hybrids. It is a medium to large shrub with lovely soft pink single flowers freely produced over a long period and dark shiny green elliptic leaves. Not easily available but worth looking for.

C. sasanqua (Japan)

This winter-flowering species has produced a number of cultivars with flowers from white through pink to red. Against a sheltered wall and under an eave it flowers progressively and from my own experience one always gets some of the blooms without frost damage.

C. sasanqua 'Liane'

Small pink flowers with pink margins. Compact habit to 1 m.

C. xwilliamsii

Produced by J. C. Williams at Caerhays Castle in Cornwall in the 1920s. *Camellia* 'J. C. Williams' is described by Hillier as perhaps the best for general planting in the British Isles. This was the first camellia I ever saw and I still consider it very good. It has partly single phlox pink flowers.

C. 'Donation'

A large semi-double orchid pink with deeper pink veining of the flowers. Regarded as perhaps the most beautiful camellia of the twentieth century. Very free-flowering. 2 m.

C. 'Barbara Clark'

A hybrid of similar parentage to the *williamsii* hybrids. Lovely semi-double flowers of rose madder pink. Robust upright bush.

Ceanothus – Californian lilac

A large genus of mainly blue-flowered shrubs, mostly evergreen. They like full sun and good drainage.

C. 'Henri Desfosse'

Deep violet-blue flowers, evergreen. 1.5 m.

C. papillosus var. *roweanus*
Dense rounded bush with dark blue flowers. Evergreen. 2 m.

Chaenomeles japonica – Ornamental quince *

Early spring-flowering shrubs with saucer shaped flowers of red, orange and white. If grown against a wall, they require pruning after flowering.

C. speciosa 'Apple Blossom' (China)
Pink flowers 1.5 m.

C. 'Mrs Murphy's Red'
Dark red flowers in late winter. 2 m.

C. 'Chochuragaki'
Large double salmon orange flowers. Good wall plant. 1.5 m.

C. 'Dr Burton'
A fine red, originating in Dunedin. Worth looking for.

Chimonanthus praecox – Winter sweet (China)*

A medium-size, easily grown shrub for a sunny situation. Small pale waxy yellow, sweetly scented flowers on leafless branches in winter. 1.5 m.

Cistus – Sun rose (Southern Europe and North Africa)

They like sunny and dry conditions and tolerate wind. Evergreen.

C. xaquilari 'Maculatus'
Large white flowers with crimson spot at base. 1.5 m.

C. 'Anne Palmer'
Clear pink flowers.

C. monspeliensis
Bushy shrub with dark green leaves and small white flowers. 50 cm.

C. 'Silver Pink'
Very hardy. 1 m.

Coprosma (New Zealand)

There are many species and cultivars of this evergreen native genus, ranging in size from ground cover to shrubs up to 2 m. There is a big variation in foliage colour, which is the main attraction, from green through gold to almost black.

C. 'Black Cloud'
Compact evergreen plant with ebony black foliage. Good ground cover.

C. 'Brunette'
Shiny olive green leaves to bronze green in winter. For a sheltered garden. 1.5 m.

C. 'Copperfield'
Copper bronze foliage all year. 1 m.

C. 'Greensleaves'
Hardy, with bright glossy green foliage all year. 1.5 m.

C. petriei
Creeping shrub, forming dense mats. Female plants have blue berries.

C. rugosa 'Clearwater Gold'
Hardy upright plant for open garden. Golden new growth. 2 m.

C. rugosa hybrid
Flat ground cover with gold hue in summer. 10 cm.

C. xkirkii 'Compacta'
Vigorous prostrate growth. Good for dry banks. 25 cm.

Cornus – Dogwood

The shrubby *Cornus* cultivars we see here are generally derived from *C. florida*, one of the best flowering dogwoods. One that has been around the longest is:

C. florida rubra*
Rosy pink bracts and reddish leaves. In flower, reminiscent of an azalea. 1.5 m.

C. florida 'Cherokee Chief'
Beautiful deep rose red bracts. 1.5 m.

Corokia (New Zealand)

An interesting native shrub genus with fine, intricate branches, small starry yellow flowers and red or orange fruits.

C. cotoneaster – korokio
Hardy evergreen low growing bush with many fine branches and small leaves. 1.5 m

C. 'Geenty's Ghost'
Bushy, grey stems and grey green leaves. 1.5 m.

C. virgata 'Red Wonder'
Very hardy, starry yellow flowered and red berries in autumn. 2 m.

Corylopsis*

An easily grown hazel-like species from Asia.

C. spicata (Japan)
This is the most available one and is a winter-flowering shrub with bright yellow flowers in racemes up to 15 cm long. 2 m.

C. willmottiae (West China)
Taller than *C. spicata* with deeper coloured foliage. Flowers soft yellow in showy racemes.

Cotoneaster (China)

Hardy ornamental shrubs, ranging from prostrate creepers to plants 2 m. or more in height. Small white flowers followed by red berries and often colourful foliage in autumn. Popular with bees.

C. dammeri 'Royal Beauty'
Good evergreen ground cover for dry banks. Orange berries in winter. 1 m spread.

C. horizontalis
Good against a wall or bank. Bright red berries. 1.5 m.

C. salicifolius
Tough medium size evergreen with brilliant red berries. Deep green foliage forms waterfall-shaped bush. 3 m.

Cytisus – Broom (Europe)

C. xkewensis
This is a most useful small shrub which fits into any garden very well. It has soft cream flowers in early summer and benefits from clipping after flowering. Very attractive. 50 cm.

Other brooms available are:
C. 'Lilac Time' – lilac pink flowers 1.5 m.
C. 'Burkwoodii' – flowers cerise crimson edged yellow 1.5 m.

Daphne

Quite a large genus of plants of which about nine species are in cultivation here. They are noted for their sweetly scented flowers and are generally small in habit.

D. blagayana (Southeast Europe)
An evergreen prostrate shrub with branches terminating in oval leaves and creamy white flowers, richly scented. Best grown in leafy soil and part shade.

D. cneorum (Central and South Europe)
A popular and beautiful little evergreen plant with rose pink scented flowers in clusters. Best in a cool moist site but with some sun. Worth the trouble once the best situation has been found. 50 cm.

D. mezereum (Europe, Asia and Siberia)*
A deciduous plant with purple red flowers. 75 cm.

D. odora (China, Japan)
Perhaps the best known of these perfumed shrubs but again trouble needs to be taken to find a site which it likes. Yellowing

of the foliage shows its displeasure. Hardy, but should be given some protection. 75 cm.

D. retusa (China)
A hardy, easy plant with red berries which will seed around. Rose purple flowers. 50 cm.

Deutzia

These are deciduous, woody plants which out of season are not so attractive but which are transformed when in flower.

D. gracilis (Japan)
A low bush of less than 1 m with beautiful white terminal clusters of flowers.

D. 'Niko'
A dwarf bush covered in white flowers in early summer. 50 cm.

Disanthus cercidifolius (Japan, China)

This is a monotypic genus (only one species in the genus). It is a moderate-sized shrub noted mainly for its beautiful crimson and claret autumn tints. It has tiny purplish flowers.

Enkianthus*

An outstanding and very distinctive small group of shrubs, only one being freely available here.

E. campanulatus (Japan)
An erect branched species up to 2.5 m. Flowers are small, cup-shaped, sulphur to rich bronze in colour which hang in profusion. Excellent autumn colour. This shrub has a 'Japanese' look and is invaluable in the garden where it creates distinction and interest.

Erica – Heaths (Europe)

These important low growing shrubs are tough, hardy and compact. Flower colour varies from white through pink, lavender to red. They prefer a neutral or acid soil (no lime) and a sunny situation. After flowering the dead inflorescences should be pruned back to maintain a tidy bush. If mass planting is planned, colours should be grouped for best effect, not mixed. All are evergreen and do well in our region.

E. carnea
There are many forms of this species with flowers from white through pink, purple and rose red. Springwood White is an old favourite.

E. cerinthoides
This is a striking South African species which I have found to be quite hardy. It has terminal clusters of long tubular crimson scarlet flowers on non branching stems.

E. xdarleyensis
This cross has resulted in a number of good plants, such as:

E. 'Darley Dale' – pink to 30 cm.
E. 'A.T.Johnson' – mauve pink to 30 cm.
E. 'Furzey' – rose purple to 30 cm.
E. 'Mary Helen' – pink to 25 cm.
E. 'Silver Beads' – Silver white flowers to 30 cm.

E. erigena (France, Spain and Northern Ireland)
E. erigena 'Nana' – deep bronze green foliage. Pink flowers in winter. 30 cm.
E. erigena 'Smokey Mauve' – dark green foliage, soft smokey pink flowers in winter. 30 cm.
E. erigena 'W.T.Ratcliff' – bright green foliage, white flowers in winter. 35 cm.

Escallonia (Chile)

A workaday evergreen shrub from South America. A wind-tolerant plant, which flowers through summer and autumn. Good for hedges. Must be pruned after flowering to maintain a tidy bush.

E. 'Apple Blossom'
Rounded shrub with glossy leaves and pink and white flowers. 1.5 m.

E. xexoniensis

Vigorous and hardy with white blush pink flowers. Well known hedging plant. 2 m.

E. macrantha rubra

Loose terminal panicles of rose crimson flowers. 2 m.

Eucryphia

These highly ornamental Southern Hemisphere shrubs should be given a place in most gardens, even a small garden (where *E. cordifolia* would not intrude). Blue Mountain Nurseries of Tapanui offer an outstanding collection of these plants where most of the species can be obtained. They are mostly evergreen and summer flowering, preferring some shelter and moist loamy soil.

E. cordifolia (Chile)

In our region, it is fairly slow-growing with grey-green slightly twisted leaves and cup-shaped white flowers with prominent stamens in summer. Evergreen.

Eucryphia xnymansensis 'Nymensay'

E. glutinosa (Chile)*

An erect deciduous large shrub or small tree with beautiful autumn tints and flowers 6 cm across.

E. lucida (Tasmania)

A densely leafy shrub or small tree with fragrant pendulous flowers up to 5 cm across. Evergreen

E. lucida 'Carousel'

Pink flowers with crimson stamens on an upright bush. Very long flowering. Evergreen.

E. xnymensensis 'Nymansay' (hybrid of two South American species)

A small to medium size tree, quite fast growing with upright habit. Beautiful cup shaped flowers 6 cm across. Evergreen.

Exochorda Pearl bush (China)

*E. racemosa**

A large spreading shrub with many racemes of large paper white flowers in early summer. Hardy.

Fothergilla (North America)*

F. major

Slow-growing shrub of medium size with white bottle brush-like flowers and brilliant autumn foliage.

Fuchsia (South America)

F. magellanica 'Mrs. Popple'

Red calyx with violet petals through summer and autumn. 1 m. Very hardy

F. magellanica var. *mollinae*

Soft pink flowers summer and autumn. Very hardy. 1–1.5 m.

Grevillea

Shrubs from Australia and Tasmania which are fairly popular in New Zealand. Only a few are hardy in our region.

G. 'Mt. Tamboritha'
This is a small flat spreading bush with soft red flowers in winter and spring. 50 cm.

G. victoriae
This is a most useful hardy shrub with rusty red flowers and long elliptic leaves. Attractive to birds and wind tolerant. Requires an annual prune. 2 m.

Hamamelis*
An erect winter flowering shrub with spidery flowers.

H. mollis – Chinese witch hazel
This was once the most popular and easily obtainable of the species and I think it is still the most attractive. Fragrant golden yellow flowers. 3 m.

Other cultivars and hybrids are available, some with fiery orange flowers, but are not as striking as H. mollis.

Hebe (New Zealand)
Like conifers, hebes are not quite as popular as they were, which is merely a cycle which many plants go through. They are useful small evergreen shrubs, filling the same role as small conifers – that is to provide form and colour the year round. The foliage is distinctive and variable with colour ranging from bronze, blue grey, olive and rich to darkest green. They don't like wet feet and prefer a drier site with some sun. To prevent them from becoming leggy and woody some need to be clipped after flowering. Blue Mountain Nurseries offer no less than 32 different species or cultivars, too many to itemise here so the more desirable and popular ones are listed. All are evergreen.

H. annulata
Bright green whipcord foliage, dwarf compact. 30 cm.

H. buchananii
Tiny sage green leaves on a low densely packed bush which spreads slowly. An attractive plant.

H. cupressoides

Rounded compact bush which has a conifer like appearance hence the name. Must be clipped lightly after flowering otherwise it becomes leggy. To 1 m.

H. cupressoides 'Nana'

A neat dwarf and rounded version of this species with tiny pale blue flowers. 40 cm.

H. hulkeana – New Zealand lilac

A much branched spreading shrub with terminal panicles of prominent lavender flowers. Requires an annual pruning. 50 cm.

H. macrantha

Upright small bush with fairly typical hebe foliage but large white flowers, (the largest of the genus). Clip or prune to prevent legginess. 75 cm.

H. ochracea 'James Stirling'

Deep bronze gold whipcord foliage. Compact spreading bush. 30 cm.

H. odora

Bright green foliage on a rounded bush. One of the better known and more desirable of the 'conventional' hebes. 75 cm.

H. pinguifolia

A round compact bush with blue-grey foliage and white flowers. 30 cm.

H. 'Red Edge'

A handsome plant with grey leaves edged in red. Mauve flowers. 60 cm.

Helichrysum (New Zealand)

There are two outstanding little shrublets from our native flora that are worth considering.

H. coralloides

This is an unusual and striking plant for the rock garden with

Hebe macrantha – largest flower of the genus

upright branchlets, the green leaves being closely adpressed with a white margin giving a somewhat coral-like effect. 30 cm

H. selago

A more conformist, compact little shrub with whipcord-like foliage. Again, the rich green leaves are adpressed to the stems showing a white margin. A very handsome plant for a small area or rock garden. 40 cm.

Hibiscus Mallow (East Asia)

Only one of these beautiful flowering shrubs is hardy enough for our region.

H. syriacus

This species flowers progressively from early to very late summer. The trumpet shaped flowers (to 6 cm) vary in colour from white through rose to red, all with a deeper red centre and the often pointed leaves are deeply toothed. It prefers a sunny site, perhaps north facing against a wall. 2 to 3 m.

Hydrangea

These are very useful hardy shrubs, usually 1.5-2 m in height. They prefer a cool position sheltered from the sun and thrive on a south or east facing wall. To produce and enhance blue flowers an acid soil is required and the addition of aluminium helps. Limy soils produce pink flowers. Pruning is necessary in early spring to remove previous season's flower shoots to within a few centimetres of the old wood. Also remove any weak growth.

Apart from a few species, most of the plants on offer are hybrids or cultivars of the *H. macrophylla* group. This contains two distinct flowering forms; the Hortensias (Mop Heads) with their bold globular, often multi-coloured flowers and the more dainty Lacecaps with flattened corymbs of flowers. What follows is a brief list from the many available.

H. macrophylla 'Blue Wave' – Lacecap*
This has large flattened heads of blue flowers surrounded by ray florets of pink to blue. This is one of the best of the Lacecaps. 1.5 m.

H. macrophylla 'Holstein' – Mop Head*
Sky blue in acid soils. 1.5 m.

H. macrophylla 'Lanarth White' – Lacecap*
Compact grower with large flattened heads of blue and pink flowers surrounded by white florets. Very good cultivar.

H. macrophylla 'Ayesha' – Silver slipper
Bold glossy green leaves and flattened dense heads of flowers like a large lilac. Lilac to pink.

H. macrophylla 'Red Star' – Mop head*
Large flattened heads of red flowers. 1.5 m.

H. villosa
A lovely late summer flowering species with large lilac to blue flowers.

Hydrangea 'Blue Wave'

Hypericum 'Hidcote Gold' (China)

A hardy summer flowering shrub of compact habit with golden yellow saucer-shaped flowers. Semi evergreen. 1.5 m

Ilex crenata 'Helleri'

A tiny holly, good for a rock garden. Green leaves and a low flattened bush. 30 cm. Hardy.

Kalmia latifolia – Calico bush (Eastern North America)

This is a rhododendron-like shrub of medium size which is not easy to site in the garden. It requires a cool moist root run with adequate drainage while the plant itself should have some sun, preferably on an east facing slope. One may ask if a plant which is so demanding, is it worth the trouble? The answer is yes.

In flower it is a most beautiful small shrub worth any amount of effort to find a place it likes. Once settled it will give no trouble and it is worth dead-heading the many seed heads it produces.

Kalmia latifolia 'Calico bush'

Flowers are deep carmine pink in bud opening to many five-sided blush pink blooms. There are other lesser species and a number of different hybrids where deeper and more dramatic colours have been produced but I believe none has the elegance of this species. Evergreen.

Kolkwitzia – Beauty bush* (China)

A graceful, very hardy plant of medium size and dense habit.

K. amabilis 'Pink Cloud'
Smothers itself with pink bell-shaped blossoms in early- to mid-summer.

Lavandula – Lavender

Hardy and useful small flowering shrubs for sunny dry sites and well-drained soils. Picked flowers remain fragrant for a long time.

L. angustifolia 'Blue Mountain'
Best in full sun and good for hedging. Blue flowers in summer . Evergreen to 40 cm.

L. xintermedia – English lavender
Deep purple or violet blue flowers in summer. Evergreen to 50 cm.

L. stoechas – French lavender
Flower colours from blue to rose lavender and pink. Can be taller growing to 80 cm. Evergreen.

Leptospermum – Manuka (New Zealand)

For many years there have been a number of colourful forms of our native manuka, ranging from dwarf plants to ones over 2 m in height. Unfortunately they have all been subject to the introduced manuka blight, a scale insect with its associated sooty mould which, while not fatal, is quite unsightly.

For this reason, these lovely shrubs seem to have lost favour. In recent years Agresearch has developed the Galaxy hybrids which are blight-resistant and easy plants to grow.

Because of the blight problem, many gardeners have been reluctant to try these new plants, which is a shame and eventually they must

Leptospermum (manuka) hybrid

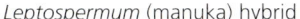

Leptospermum (manuka) hybrid

resurface again. I have two of these blight-free hybrids which have lush bushy foliage and colourful flowers. They are well worth a place in the garden.

Lonicera – Honeysuckles

Shrubby honeysuckles, distinct from the climbing species are very hardy and easily grown in any ordinary soil. They need to be thinned and cut back after flowering to a few centimetres of the old wood.

> *L. korolkowii** (Turkestan)
> A graceful arching shrub with pink flowers followed by red berries. 1.5 m.

> *L. nitida* (China)
> Fine leaved evergreen with sweetly scented flowers. Responds well to trimming. 2 m.

Lophomyrtus (New Zealand)

This evergreen shrub is grown for its foliage form and colour making it a good foil for other plants. It has small almond pink flowers in the leaf axils followed by red berries. The foliage is useful for flower arranging.

L. xralphii 'Kathryn'

A hybrid Myrtus with deep red oval leaves. 2 m.

L. xralphii 'Variegata'

Small leaves, green with cream edges in winter followed by a pink blush. 2 m.

Lupinus – Lupin

From the Mackenzie Country through the Lindis highway, there is plenty of evidence in our part of the country of what the Russell lupin (*Lupinus polyphyllus* hybrids) is capable of. It is easily grown and colourful but its prolific seeding is extremely hard to eradicate and in the garden it has to be regarded as something of a weed. Historically, seed, which is 2000 years old has been found to be still viable!

Magnolia

The *Magnolia* genus has already been dealt with under trees but there are two which do not exceed about 3 m bringing them into the shrub category.

M. liliiflora (Central China)

This has slender tulip-like flowers, flushed purple on the outside, creamy white within. To 3 m.

M. loebneri 'Leonard Messel'

This is a very fine hybrid with pink star-shaped flowers. It is one of the hardiest magnolias. To 3 m.

Nandina (India, China and Japan)

An unusual monotypic genus which looks something like a bamboo but is related to *Berberis*. Needs shelter and full sun. Evergreen.

N. domestica – Heavenly bamboo

Attractive bamboo-like small shrub with colourful gold and orange foliage. Small white flowers in terminal panicles in summer. 1 m.

Olearia (New Zealand)

Very hardy native shrubs, more likely to appeal to those who appreciate a rugged plant. They cannot be regarded as ornamental except by the native plant purist but they are valuable as windbreak shelter. They are evergreen, some with holly-like foliage and have white daisy flowers in summer.

Osmanthus

I have grown this shrub in more than one garden and can highly recommend it. The species that is most popular is:

O. delavayi (China)
A very attractive small-leaved plant, hardy and easily grown in most soils. It has masses of small fragrant creamy flowers in spring and should be considered for most gardens. Evergreen, 1–1.5 m.

Pachystegia insignis – Marlborough rock daisy (New Zealand)

This large-flowered native daisy is an excellent garden plant. It occurs in rocky places and cliff faces in the Kaikoura region but surprisingly does equally well in our district. It has large white aster-like flowers up to 7cm across and handsome rich green foliage with white felted underside. 50 cm.

Paeonia – Tree paeonies*

There are two species which are freely available while a third is worth searching for. They require well-drained soil and are gross feeders but will survive in ordinary soil.

P. delavayi (China)
Deep red flowers with golden filaments. Good foliage. 1.5 m.

P. lutea 'Ludlowii' (Tibet)
Bears single bright yellow flowers up to 7.5 cm across with similar foliage to *P. delavayi*.

P. suffruticosa (China)

This is the original wild tree paeony from which so many cultivars have been raised. Flowers palest flesh pink to silver white. Many named cultivars of different colours are available with flowers up to 15 cm or more across. 1.8 m.

Penstemon (Northwestern America and Mexico)

These sub-shrubs are evergreen and include a number of excellent species and some larger hybrids with flowers of apple blossom pink to red which last through summer. The smaller species, some of which are suitable for the rock garden have spring flowers of brilliant blue through purple to pink. The best of them can be had from the alpine and perennial nurseries.

Philadelphus – Mock orange

P. 'Beauclerk'*

Large white single flowers with cerise centre in summer. Fragrant and hardy. 1.5 m.

P. 'Frosty Morn-Bride's Blossom'

Fragrant double white flowers. Very hardy. 1.5 m.

P. 'Manteau d'Hermine'

Compact bush, creamy double white flowers, fragrant. 1 m.

P. 'Virginal-Bride's Blossom'

Strong growing erect shrub with double white flowers. Most popular of the group. 2–3 m.

Phormium tenax – New Zealand flax (New Zealand)

Our native flax grows to a considerable size (up to 2 m) making a dense impenetrable shrub. Good for shelter in exposed and damp situations. There are a number of smaller growing plants with narrower sword-like leaves and interesting bi-colour variations which make them useful landscape plants in the right setting.

Photinia (Asia)

This evergreen is more of a 'work-horse' plant than an ornamental one although the new foliage is attractive. It is useful for shelter or hedging.

P. xfraseri 'Red Robin'

This plant, raised in New Zealand, has spectacular sharply toothed glossy green foliage and brilliant red young growths. Trim in late summer. 3 m.

P. xfraseri 'Robusta'

Strong growing, with coppery red young growths. Trim in late summer. 3 m.

Pieris

These are *Rhododendron*-like shrubs which require similar conditions. Avoid direct exposure to the sun – part shade preferred. Evergreen.

P. forrestii 'Wakehurst' (China)

A tall shrub with brilliant red new growth and panicles of lily-of-the-valley like creamy white flowers. 2–3 m.

P. japonica (Japan)

There are a number of varieties of this species, mostly with white flowers and some with pink. They grow to about 1 m.

Potentilla*

Small woody deciduous shrubs which are very hardy and thrive in any soil. They tolerate full sun or part shade.

P. dahurica 'Manchu'

A charming little dwarf plant with tiny grey green leaves and attractive white flowers over a long period in summer. 50 cm.

P. fruticosa

This species has produced a lot of hybrids with varying flower colours but the type plant has sage green foliage and bright yellow flowers for several months through summer.

Both are worthy garden plants.

Rhododendron

Of all flowering shrubs, the rhododendron is probably the most important. It has the greatest diversity of flower, form and foliage even exceeding the camellia in this respect. There are between 400–500 species in the wild, from tiny prostrate alpines to large trees. Asia, and China in particular, holds the greatest concentration of rhododendrons with a distinct family of sub-tropical species coming from New Guinea and Malaysia.

This vast array has enabled hybridizers to produce thousands of cultivars, bred for new colours and more importantly hardiness. But with many hybrids the distinctive character of the species' parents is often lost.

In the Lakes District and Central Otago, rhododendrons do reasonably well despite conditions that are far from ideal. Their preference is for a moist atmosphere, good rainfall and acid soil. None of these elements is present but good soil drainage is and rhododendrons appreciate this.

Rhododendron campylogynum

In our generally neutral soils, mineral deficiencies affect some rhododenrons and this has to be dealt with. In areas which have acid soil (and there are a few) the plants tend to be very healthy.

Leaves are a barometer of a plant's health. Curling or blackening of the leaf margins may indicate wind burn or over exposure to the sun. Brown patches on the leaf undersides are caused by powdery mildew for which there is no treatment other than removal of the affected leaves. It is not usually fatal in our colder climate. Yellowing (chlorosis) suggests mineral deficiency or an alkaline soil.

Treatment for unhealthy plants may include a dressing of magnesium sulphate or a liquid solution of NITROSOL, a blood and bone concentrate plus key minerals. Mulching with compost retains moisture but adding fertilizer is not usually necessary as rhododendrons are low nutrition plants. Acid soil is what they really like.

Atmospheric dryness is the main problem and rhododendrons should be given overhead protection from direct sun to alleviate this.

There is a great range of hybrids which can be bought in flower, making personal preference easy. The main check should be for bud hardiness. Early flowering plants are best avoided because of frost damage.

Rhododendron 'Crest'

The species can be more interesting and are often the most beautiful. Listed below are a few which I have grown in our garden here and which provide variety to the run-of-the-mill hybrids.

R. augustinii (China, Tibet)
Slender small-leaved upright shrub with open flat lavender-blue flowers with prominent stamens. A beautiful species. 2 m.

R. campylogynum (China, Tibet)
This is a dinky little compact dwarf with small shiny leaves and thimble-shaped flowers. Colour varies from plum purple to deep salmon. Needs shade. 40 cm.

R. davidsonianum (China)
Belonging to the same group (Triflorum) as *R. augustinii* it is very similar in appearance. However, the leaves are narrower and the flowers are a lovely clear pink of varying intensity. 2 m.

R. hippophaeoides (China)
The name may be a mouthful but its small-leaved densely clad habit and masses of small lavender-blue flowers make this a desirable plant. Hardy and easy with aromatic foliage. 1 m.

Rhododendron davidsonianum 'Exbury Pink'

R. nakaharae (Taiwan)

This is a dwarf prostrate azalea with dense woody habit and brick red flowers. Part sun only.

R. occidentale (Northwest America)

A great success in our region where the climate seems to suit it. Flowers creamy white to pale pink with yellow or orange basal blotch. A form known as 'Delicatissima' has particularly colourful flowers. Good autumn foliage colour. 1.5 m.

R. radicans (Tibet)

A tiny prostrate alpine with flat rose purple flowers, large for the size of the bush and tiny leaves. A rock garden specimen requiring some protection from sun in our climate.

R. schlippenbachii (Korea, Manchuria)

A very beautiful deciduous azalea with quite large single flowers of softest pink. Needs part shade.

R. yakushimanum (Japan)

A most unusual species with deep green leathery recurved leaves on a densely packed small bush. Compact flower trusses opening

Rhododendron occidentale

blush pink fading eventually to white. Very hardy and popular worldwide. 50 cm.

R. 'Crest'

A medium to larger hybrid with large trusses of clear primrose flowers. One of Lionel de Rothschild's triumphs.

R. 'Scarlet King Kaka'

Brilliant scarlet flowers on a medium-sized bush. One of Edgar Stead's hybrids raised in Christchurch from the 1950s.

For those interested in growing the species and more interesting hybrids, the Dunedin Rhododendron Group issues a comprehensive list of species and hybrids each year. Details are listed under 'Plant Sources' at the end of this book.

Rosa – Roses

Roses have been cultivated for a very long time, firstly by the Romans and later in the Middle East before being introduced into Europe around the 13th century. They grow in the wild in all parts of the Northern

Rhododendron 'Scarlet King Kaka'

Hemisphere and in recent centuries have been developed by breeders to produce a hugely diverse range of plants.

In compiling this list of hardy shrubs I have to admit that the rose is my 'Achilles Heel'. Fortunately my wife grew roses for some years and I became interested, more as an observer than a grower. In the process I came to realize that the rose must be the most beautiful flower of all and that what stops it from being the supreme flowering shrub is the fact it is deciduous, has to be pruned back annually and needs a lot more work and attention than others.

As regards care and cultivation there is quite a lot to learn, more than can be dealt with here, but there are excellent specialist works to refer to. Among many, we have *Roses* by Roger Phillips and Martyn Rix (Pan Garden Plant Series), which, with good cultural notes and 1400 beautiful colour plates suits the average gardener very well.

In our garden we grew several shrub roses, a number of climbers and better known hybrids. Here are some worth mentioning:

R. banksiae 'Lutea'

Vigorous almost rampant climber with no thorns. Small double creamy yellow flowers. Useful for growing up a tree.

R. 'Bantry Bay'

Beautiful semi-double flowers of soft pink. Great over an arch or pergola.

R. 'Bloomfield's Courage'

A vigorous rambler, good on a fence. Small single cherry red flowers.

R. 'Claire Matin'

Attractive irregular double soft to medium pink. Can be a floribunda or climber.

R. 'Complicata'

An old hybrid with single flowers up to 10 cm across. Soft rose pink, white centre and golden filaments.

R. 'Constance Spry'
Slow-growing David Austin rose with full double scented pink flowers. Very showy but flowers once only and may be a shrub or climber.

R. 'Double Delight'
Hybrid tea rose, red with cream centre. Delicious scent 1.3 m.

R. 'Dublin Bay'
Brilliant red climber and rambler. Excellent on a fence. No scent.

R. 'Dupontii'
Beautiful cream white flowers with golden filaments, up to 7 cm across. To 2 m.

R. 'Golden Wings'
Sweetly scented single flowers, cream deepening to gold with golden filaments over a long period. A magnificent rose. To 2 m.

R. 'Iceberg'
One of the most popular white roses. Can be a climber or floribunda with full double flowers of purest white. As a floribunda 2–3 m, or 5 m as a climber.

R. 'Margaret Merrill'
A very beautiful semi-double white with deeper centre, strong scent and medium height.

R. 'Meg'
A floribunda or climber with single flowers of an exquisite pale apricot and deeper coloured filaments. Once flowering. To 4 m.

R. 'Mutabilis'
A shrub up to 2.5 m with bronze young leaves and flowers opening yellow, then pink and lastly crimson.

R. 'Nancy Hayward'
Vigorous spreading climber with large cerise-scarlet flowers, which positively glow.

Rosa 'Meg'

Rosa 'Nancy Hayward'

Rosa 'Sally Holmes'

Rosa 'Sparrieshoop'

R. 'Sally Holmes'

This is a hybrid Musk Rose with flowers on tall growing shoots. Slightly floppy single pale pink to apricot blooms with repeat flowering. 1.3 m.

R. 'Sparrieshoop'

A mid-summer bloomer with flowers salmon pink. Upright and open, best on a pillar.

R. 'Seagull'

A vigorous climber with large corymbs of small semi-double scented flowers of creamy white with golden filaments.

Rosmarinus officinalis – Common rosemary

R. 'Benenden Blue'

Blue flowers through summer on low evergreen spreading bush. Needs sun. 50 cm.

R. 'Lady in White'

White flowers in summer on upright bushy plant. Prune. 1 m.

R. 'Lockwood de Forest' – Weeping rosemary

For rock walls and banks. Lavender flowers and aromatic perfume. Evergreen 30 cm

R. 'Tuscan Blue' – Upright rosemary

Bright blue flowers and fragrant leaves. Can be used as a cooking herb or for pot pourri. Evergreen 1 m.

Syringa – Lilacs*

Hardy deciduous shrubs which produce fragrant flowers in midsummer. Not particular as to soil, and enjoy sun.

S. laciniata

Fragrant lilac-pink flowers on bushy shrub with finely-cut leaves. 1 m.

S. microphylla 'Superba'

A small bushy shrub with pinkish red flowers in spring. 1.5 m.

S. × persica – Persian lilac

A rounded bushy plant with slender branches covered in small lilac flowers. 1.5 m.

Viburnum

This is a large genus of easily grown evergreen and deciduous shrubs which includes some of the best flowering woody plants in cultivation. Brilliant autumn colours are a feature of some of the deciduous species. Blue Mountain Nurseries offer over 30 different species and cultivars, all worth looking at. Here are four of the most popular:

V. ×burkwoodii

Medium-sized semi-evergreen shrub with pink-budded fragrant white flowers in tight rounded trusses. To 2 m.

V. carlesii

One of the best Viburnums for its sweetly scented flowers, rounded habit and downy leaves. To 1.5 m.

V. plicatum Mariesii

Beautiful new heavily veined foliage and rather spreading habit with creamy white flowers which give the appearance of a snow laden bush. A great favourite.

V. tinus 'Laurustinus'

This evergreen *Viburnum* is a hardy and easy plant, resistant to wind, heat and cold. As well as being ornamental, with white tinged pink flowers in winter it provides useful low level shelter. To 1.5 m.

Weigela

Very hardy shrubs with narrowly open tubular flowers.

W. florida (Japan, Korea, China)
Soft pink flowers in spring. 1.5 m.

W. praecox (Japan, Korea, Manchuria)
Large honey-scented pink flowers in early summer. 1.5 m.

Perennials

Having worked our way down through large trees to lesser ones and shrubs, both large and small, we come to the perennials, which can be very tiny to a considerable size.

They provide the finishing touches to a garden already well-planted with trees and shrubs. Without them there would be a lack of balance and bareness where there should be flourishing growth. Many of them disappear in winter and I have an ongoing problem of planting other things on top of them, only to be discovered in the spring. Despite careful labelling, the birds are forever tossing labels out of the ground so care must be taken to have the labels deeply inserted into the soil beside the plants.

Perennials are diverse in every way, in size, form and colour. Choice must therefore be varied to suit a particular garden and this is where the gardener's skill must come to the fore. For example, in an herbaceous border, some of the taller ones such as *Delphinium*, *Astilbe*, *Paeonia*, *Platycodon* and *Thalictrum* can be used as background planting with lower growing plants in the front. The really small perennials are better sited in a rock garden, raised bed, or otherwise dedicated small area where their welfare is more easily checked on.

The list which follows includes plants which require widely differing situations from cool moist to open dry. It is essential to know their requirements before planting.

AGAPANTHUS (South Africa)

This genus is grown here but it is more usually seen in coastal areas where it does well.

A. orientalis – Nile lily

This is the most common species along with its many cultivars of varying shades of pink, violet and blue. A good one is 'Blue Nile' which has massive heads of mauve flowers. As they are large plants, they may look their best at the back of a wild herbaceous border. They are evergreen and will grow in any well drained soil. Sun.

Alchemilla mollis – Lady's mantle
(Balkans, Russia and Turkey)

This plant is good for the front of a border. It has kidney-shaped leaves and small greenish yellow flowers. Winter dormant. 30 cm.

Alstroemeria (South America)

These hardy plants are pleasantly colourful in a border and provide a popular cut flower. There are some 50 species from alpines (10 cm) to more vigorous ones, up to 1 m tall. They grow from rhizomes that bear fleshy tubers, and the clumps tend to expand gradually, ultimately requiring to be checked.

Flowers are in soft shades of apricot, cream and deep rose often with a deeper throat or blotch with speckling. They are hardy and will grow in any soil.

Alstroemeria hybrid

Althaea – Hollyhock

A background plant for the herbaceous border as it can reach 2 m in height. It imparts a 'cottage' feel to the garden when in full bloom and is worthwhile in the right situation. Winter dormant.

There are both single and double-flowered cultivars mostly derived from *A. rosea*. Colours vary from white, cream, pink through to red, scarlet and maroon. Any soil is satisfactory along with good drainage.

Anemone

There is a large number of species but only a few are common garden plants. All winter-dormant. The most popular are:

A. blanda (Greece)

Low growing with single starry blue flowers in spring. They will increase by seeding around if planted in a cool moist spot. There are deep violet-blue, pink and white forms also, which are less freely available.

A. xfulgens (Crete)

This has been in our garden once or twice and we were taken aback by the brilliant red of the flowers. They were so bright thta the plants had to be shifted away from other flowers to avoid the distraction. A lovely anemone nevertheless.

A. japonica – Japanese anemone

The single white flowers on tall stems are very attractive but this anemone has woody rhizomes that travel quite quickly, with new plants popping up everywhere. It is extremely difficult to get rid of and is better planted where little else is being grown.

A. nemorosa – Woodland anemone (Europe)

We have seen this in the Scottish highlands growing under native oak trees. It is a lovely spring-flowering plant spreading fairly quickly into large patches by its thin brittle rhizomes. It is quite controllable. Colour varies from white to powder blue, soft yellow and pink.

A. obtusiloba patula (Himalaya)
A small and beautiful species which produces a few buttercup-like flowers of soft blue.

A. sylvestris (Europe)
Attractive single white flowers on long stems. Moist conditions in semi-shade.

Aquilegia – Granny's bonnet
There are many species and hybrids of this attractive summer-green perennial. All seed freely around the garden but they shouldn't be ruled out because of this. Remove dead flower heads before seeding takes place. The few smaller species we have are more suitable for the rock garden.

A. bertolonii (European Alps)
A beautiful little plant up to 15 cm tall with violet-blue flowers. It seeds hardly at all and if it does seedlings are valued.

A. canadensis (North America)
A striking species with scarlet flowers tipped yellow. Seedlings should be kept. 30–40 cm.

Aquilegia canadensis

A. flabellata (Japan)

A lovely little plant with mauve blue flowers tipped white.

Most of the hybrids are taller growing up to 70–80 cm and have long spurred flowers in various shades – all attractive. They all seed vigorously.

Armeria – Thrift (Europe)

A. maritima – Sea thrift

The most common of these tufted plants, it is useful in the rockery or border growing from 15–30 cm high with flowers white, pink or purplish rose.

Aster – Michaelmas daisy

From the very large number of species there are a few which can be an attractive addition to a rockery or border.

A. alpinus (European Alps)
Large flowers of violet-blue. To 20 cm.

A. farreri (China and Tibet)
Another handsome daisy having large violet-purple flowers with orange discs. Low-growing.

Astilbe (Asia, North America)

Astilbe have tall plumes or spikes of flowers with colours varying from white through pink to wine shades and attractive fern-like foliage. They make good border plants but like moist – even boggy – conditions, plus some compost for long life.

Bergenia – Elephant's ears

They belong to the saxifrage family and can be recognized as an oversized member of such when in flower. Fleshy leaves and 30 cm tall panicles of flowers, pink to varying shades of rose and red.

Campanula – Harebell

A very useful group of summer flowering plants, which include many lovely species. Most are small and low growing and some tend to spread by stolons but can be checked easily enough. Flower colour may be white but is predominately blue from palest porcelain blue to deep violet. Hardy and easy.

C. betulaefolia (Armenia)
A small campanula with pointed birch-like leaves and white bell-shaped flowers.

C. carpatica 'Elaine' (Carpathian Mts)
A ground-hugging plant with masses of pale lavender flowers. A favourite of mine.

C. cochlearifolia (European Alps)
One of the best known of the campanulas, with little thimble shaped flowers, which can be white to shades of blue.

C. garganica (Italy)
Arching sprays of star shaped blue flowers.

C. rotundifolia – European harebell
Although this is the common harebell it is well worth growing. It is a light and airy plant with attractive lavender-blue bell flowers.

There are many other campanulas, which are worth growing if one gets interested in these excellent perennials.

Cheiranthus – Wallflower

This old-fashioned plant, remembered from childhood is still worth considering for a background against a wall or fence. It is more likely to be biennial and seed must be sown for continuity. Colours vary from white, yellow, orange, bronze and red.

Chionodoxa – Glory of the snow (Turkey)

A wonderful little bulbous plant, which should be in every spring garden. It enjoys our cold winters and good drainage, increasing quite rapidly. In two or three years we have been able to spread the bulbs around making a great show in late September and early October. Friends have benefitted too.

C. gigantea
This species has larger and more dramatic flowers than *C. luciliae*. Lovely sky blue with a white centre and narrow strap shaped leaves.

Chrysanthemum mawii (Morocco)

This is a low-growing plant with small pink flowers about 2.5 cm across with a dark centre and attractive deeply cut grey-green foliage. A popular plant which should be in every garden.

Delphinium – Larkspur

In our cold climate this seems to be perennial. The tall flower spikes are usually pale to azure and violet-blue, sometimes white and usually require staking or support. Best as a background plant in the border.

Dianthus (Europe)

Dianthus caryophyllus is the species from which comes the carnation as we know it. From this has sprung a great range of cultivars and hybrids of varying size and colour. There are also some lovely small species which come from the European Alps which can be obtained from the alpine and perennial nurseries. These make fine rock garden specimens and are recommended.

Diascia (South Africa)

Quite pretty little plants flowering from mid to late summer.

D. 'Ruby Field'
Possibly the best Diascia, a hybrid with nemesia-like flowers of tangerine-rose. 25 cm.

Digitalis purpurea – Common foxglove

A plant which, in the right situation, can enhance an herbaceous border or cottage garden. There is a wide range of shades from pale pink to deep red. It will reach to 1.8 m in height.

Epimedium

A good border plant of modest size with attractive heart-shaped foliage and small flowers of white, orange, red or yellow.

E. niveum (Japan)
A white-flowered species, compact to about 20 cm.

E. ×warleyense
Light green leaves and coppery red flowers to 30 cm.

Eranthis hyemalis – Winter aconite (Europe)

A favourite harbinger of spring. Low-growing, it has clusters of brilliant buttercup yellow flowers in early September and is one of the first flowers to appear after the winter. It does seed quite freely but gardening friends usually welcome a gift of seeds.

Erythronium – Dog's tooth violet

These are very beautiful bulbous plants preferring a moist site although E. 'White Beauty' will stand some sun. We have E. *hendersonii* and E. *revolutum* in a partly shaded area of the rock garden. All erythroniums have heavily reflexed petals.

E. dens-canis (Europe, Asia and Japan)
The leaves are beautifully marbled purple and brown. Flowers usually purplish rose although other colour forms are available.

E. revolutum (North America)
Lovely soft pink pendant flowers on variable height stems

E. 'White Beauty'
Easiest, best known and equally as attractive in a less delicate way, it has many large creamy flowers with heavily reflexed petals, which make a wonderful display. Bulbs increase quite quickly.

Erythronium revolutum

Gentiana

These vividly blue-flowered plants conjure up visions of distant snow capped ranges. Walking in the mountains of Switzerland and Austria it is exciting to see them growing prolifically in high alpine pasture often grazed by a few cattle.

The later flowering Asiatic gentians come mainly from China and Tibet and are equally desirable. These have been crossed with each other to produce some outstanding colours from vivid copper sulphate to Cambridge blue as well as deeper richer ones.

Good true blue flowers stand out in any garden and have a special fascination for all gardeners. Only the Himalayan poppy, *Meconopsis betonicifolia* and *M. grandis,* can challenge the gentian. All are supremely beautiful plants.

G. acaulis (Europe)
The well known spring gentian has velvety flowers of rich royal blue. Needs composty and gritty soil to flower well. *G. alpina* is a smaller version of *G. acaulis*. Don't allow to dry out in summer.

Gentiana acaulis – growing above Grindelwald, Switzerland

G. 'Drake's Strain'

Originating at Jack Drake's Nursery at Inschriach in Scotland many years ago, this famous Asiatic hybrid has large Cambridge blue trumpets. Southwell Plants at Hillend produce vigorous plants available through the markets. It must have a cool moist root run through summer and rich composty soil.

G. 'Southwell Super'

Another autumn-flowering gentian developed by Southwell Plants. Large upright deep blue trumpets. Keep cool and moist through summer.

G. *saxosa* (New Zealand)

One of our native species, it forms a tight mat with upward-facing white bell flowers. Gritty soil.

G. *septemfida* (Asia and Caucasus)

A taller growing mid-summer gentian. Deep blue trumpets on 15 cm stems. Some sun. Easy.

There are various other Asiatic gentians, all of them good. In our region all need to be looked after through summer. Choosing a good site is crucial.

Gentiana 'Drake's Strain'

Geranium himalayense

Geranium

Of the 400 species there are only a few to be considered here.

G. dalmaticum
A small growing open plant with soft pink flowers. 25 cm.

G. himalayense
This has heads of large blue saucer-shaped flowers on a small bush to 45 cm. A favourite.

There are a few other good species such as *G. cinerium* (deep cerise flowers) and *G. wallichianum* 'Buxton's Blue' if they can be obtained.

Geum

Geums are attractive and agreeable plants to have in the garden. They like a damp situation and merge in well with other plants.

G. chilense (Chile)
It has flower stems up to 45 cm and colours from orange red to purplish red. Hardy.

G. coccinea
Similar in habit to *G. chilense* with flowers tangerine orange.

Gladiolus

Currently there seems to be limited interest in *Gladiolus* but they are nevertheless well known to all gardeners and flower lovers. Flower colour can be brilliant and often multi-coloured. You either like them or you don't. However, there is one species which is dainty and subtle and would look at home anywhere.

G. tristis (Natal)
It is hardy, has fine reedy foliage and pale yellow trumpets about 3 cm across. It grows to about 60 cm in height and increases quite steadily. Easily divided to give away to friends.

Gypsophila (Europe)

Much favoured by florists who like its airy foliage and tiny flowers to complement a bouquet.

G. paniculata
Sprays of tiny white flowers. Also a double-flowered form 'Flore Pleno'. To 60 cm.

G. repens 'Rosea'
A lovely dwarf plant with pink flowers in early summer. To 15 cm.

Haberlea ferdinandi-coburgii (Balkans)

Although vaguely reminiscent of a primula it doesn't belong to this genus. It forms clumps of thick textured toothed leaves with umbels of 2–4 tubular flowers, lilac on the outside and paler within. Well grown, it is a first class garden plant. Does best in the shade of a small tree such as a maple.

Helleborus – Winter rose (Europe, Asia)

One of the few winter-flowering plants, hellebores have an important place in the year round garden. They date back 2000 years and were known to the ancient Greeks. The roots have been experimented with for medicinal purposes but are best known for their toxic properties.

From the 15 species, which originate mainly from the Balkans and Turkey, large numbers of cultivars and hybrids have been produced. Flower colours are usually subtle, white ranging through dusky pink, occasional creams and soft yellows and very deep purple. They are gross feeders and being a winter plant, not troubled by drying out.

H. 'White Magic' (*orientalis* ×*niger*)

This plant was raised by Pat Stuart of Wanaka and has been very popular. A clear white with large flat open flowers well displayed. (It does seed prolifically.)

H. 'Moonshine' ('White Magic' ×*sternii*)

Another hellebore raised by Pat Stuart, it has soft yellow flowers.

H. *orientalis* hybrids

These are offered in a variety of shades from white and pink to purple with degrees of speckling.

Heuchera (North America)

A good front-of-border plant with dense fleshy-leaved habit and flower stems with loose panicles of tiny flowers. 45 cm.

H. *micrantha* 'Palace Purple'

A coppery leaved form with white flowers.

H. *sanguinea* (Arizona and N.Mexico)

Deep rosy pink flowers.

After a year or so the plants may need to be broken up and replanted as they can become congested.

Hosta

Grown mainly for their large attractive leaves of rich green and blue green colours often strongly variegated they require cool moist conditions, even on the margins of bogs and pools. Some achieve considerable height and width so these measurements need to be known before purchasing.

H. 'Halcyon'
Blue grey leaves and corymbs of violet flowers in late summer.
30 cm.

H. sieboldii 'Elegans' (Japan)
Bluish leaves and white flowers make a clump. to 30 x 35 cm.

H. sieboldii 'Alba'
Bright green leaves and white flowers loosely displayed. 30 cm.

For those who like variegated foliage, leaves can be green with
gold edging or vice versa. Many other species and hybrids are
available which are best chosen on inspection whilst checking
on ultimate size.

Iberis – Candytuft

This is a great little sub-shrub or perennial with vivid white flowers in
spring. Oddly enough it is omitted from several plant manuals but is
included in an excellent book on alpines! That is strange as it has long
been a popular plant in our gardens.

I. sempervirens (Mediterranean Europe)
We have an old specimen of this evergreen *Iberis* which produces
its pure white flowers in attractive racemes. At 10 years old it is
1 m across by 40 cm high.

I. sempervirens 'Little Gem'
Reaching only 12 cm in height this is a good plant for a rock
garden.

Incarvillea Pride of China

An unusual winter dormant plant with quite large flattened trumpet
flowers 5 cm or more across.

I. delavayi 'Bees Pink'
This is a form with rosy pink flowers, not such a hard colour as
the normal species. Pinnate fern-like foliage. A white form is
also available.

Iris

This genus of plants is vast and can be a little intimidating unless one is an iris specialist. The tiniest is a mere 10 cm or so tall while the bearded irises may reach 90 cm. There are about six distinct groups each displaying special characteristics.

The Xiphion Group contains the 'English, Dutch and Spanish' irises which have narrow leaves and more open flowers and falls than the bearded iris. Many colours.

Juno Group (Middle East)

I. bucharica
A dwarf plant with fleshy leaves and yellow and white flowers.

I. ×sindpur
Beautiful porcelain blue flowers tinted sea green with small yellow blotch.

Reticulata Group

A favourite iris, they can be rock garden subjects or may be planted in an area with good drainage where they can be checked and not overgrown.

I. histrioides (Turkey)
Very dwarf, to 12 cm with soft blue and lavender flowers in late July and early August. Our plants increase quite steadily. Very worthwhile.

I. reticulata (Caucasus)
The type plant has narrow petalled flowers of rich heliotrope with a small yellow blotch. Also available are named varieties in shades from pale blue to deepest royal blue and violet purple. A wonderful bulb to have in the garden.

Bearded *Iris*

They require care and management along with alkaline soil and no animal manure. Most readily available are the dwarfer varieties which do well and include some good soft blues, lavenders, bronze and white.

Iris reticulata 'Royal Blue'

They enhance any border. Plants have to be lifted, cleaned and replanted to get rid of couch grass which infiltrates the rhizomes.

Evansia Group – Crested *Iris*

I. cristata (North America)
A delightful little dwarf plant about 13 cm high with flowers either clear lavender blue with white eye or 'Alba', a white form.

There are one or two other groups and many more species of iris that can't be dealt with here and are more likely to be of interest to the specialist grower.

Lavatera – Mallow

This is a plant which falls between shrubs and perennials. The one below is perhaps more of a shrub although it has been described as one or the other.

L. 'Barnsley'
A beautiful variety, fairly recently introduced with pale pink flowers fading to deeper pink. Tolerates hot dry situations and requires pruning. 2 m.

Lilium

The lilies come from the temperate regions of the Northern Hemisphere and the prime requirement for growing them is perfect drainage, which we are fortunate to have in our region.

L. auratum (Japan)
These beautiful lilies vary in colour from a speckled white with a thin pale yellow streak to deeper shades of pink. It is not easy, requiring perfect drainage and likes to be sited amongst low shrubs.

L. regale – Christmas Lily (China)
A hardy and popular lily with large funnel-shaped flowers, lilac outside with yellow throat on long stems. 1.8 m.

L. speciosum

Another popular and well known lily with speckled deep wine coloured flowers and heavily reflexed petals. Autumn flowering.

L. mackliniae

This small lesser known lily is fairly reliable. It has small bell shaped flowers of blush white or soft pink. Named by the great plant explorer Frank Kingdon Ward for his wife Joyce Macklin.

There are numerous hybrid lilies in various attractive colours, all well worth growing. Most are best planted among other non-competing small shrubs to give them a cool root run.

Lithodora (Europe)

A lovely ground or wall-hugging plant with small grey-green leaves and small gentian blue flowers. It is very popular and seen in many gardens. It needs some sun but not too dry a position. Trim occasionally.

Lychnis – Campion

These plants have been seen flowering and growing wild near Macetown, suggesting they were introduced by the early gold miners.

L. flos-jovis

Bright cerise flowers and woolly silver foliage. 60 cm.

L. coronaria 'Alba'

Another species which looks well in the border. It has attractive four petalled white flowers and grows to 60 cm.

Meconopsis – Himalayan poppy

As mentioned previously true blue flowers have always held a fascination for gardeners but there are only a few. The blue meconopsis is one and it is hard to exaggerate the beauty and appeal of these plants. Although in our region they will only survive in a microclimate, I for one keep on growing and losing them. They are mostly monocarpic or at best biennial but they produce plenty of seed and can be kept going in this way.

Lilium mackliniae

They grow extremely well in Scotland and it is here I have seen them thriving in a way we can't emulate in New Zealand. Nevertheless most keen gardeners have had periodic triumphs. In Wanaka and Wakatipu there are odd pockets of peaty soil and moist conditions that suit them. Otherwise it is a challenge but an exciting and rewarding one.

M. betonicifolia

Seedlings vary in colour a little but the best have typical sky blue flowers a little smaller than M. grandis and M. sheldonii.

M. grandis

Magnificent large nodding flowers of deeper blue.

M. 'Lingholm'

A tall plant of recent introduction, reputed to be perennial rather than monocarpic. Magnificent large flowers of rich sky blue.

M. ×sheldonii (M. betonicafolia ×grandis)

This famous beautiful large-flowered hybrid was made by W. G. Sheldon in England, in 1934. Deep sky blue.

M. quintuplinerva – Farrer's harebell poppy

This is one we can grow here. It is a deciduous perennial with small narrow leaves and nodding lavender bells from basal scapes. Flower stems up to 30 cm or more. It is quite different from its larger brethren both in size and colour but beautiful nevertheless. For a number of years it has been in our garden where it enjoys a cool moist site and fertile soil.

There are a number of other desirable species, rarely obtainable, amongst which I must mention:

M. integrifolia

Golden yellow lamp shade flowers from lovely hairy leaved pale green rosettes.

M. punicea

Perhaps the most sensational of all the meconopsis. A small plant with hanging flag-like flowers of crimson scarlet.

Both of the above are monocarpic. *M. punicea* is particularly difficult as it is necessary to cross-pollinate two plants to get viable seed to keep it going.

Meconopsis 'Lingholm'

Mertensia

A plant which belongs to the forget-me-not family with greyish blue spatulate leaves and umbels of small blue flowers. A few of the species are small enough for the rock garden. One purchased as *M. asiatica* was a good winter dormant plant but the name was suspect. If obtainable, any are worth looking at.

Muscari – Grape hyacinth (Europe, Asia)

Closely related to the *Hyacinth* group, they are hardy spring-flowering bulbs, ideal for the rock garden. There are at least three worth mentioning.

M. armeniacum

The common grape hyacinth. Cobalt blue flowers.

M. azureum

Dense heads of miniature bells of azure blue. Early flowering.

M. botryoides

Dwarf, with spikes of sky blue flowers. Equally desirable is the white form 'Album'.

Narcissus

Fortunately we don't seem to be affected by the *Narcissus* fly, eel worm or basal rot, due perhaps to free draining soil and a hard climate. The Narcissus species are all beautiful plants. Here are a few of the better known ones:

N. bulbocodium – Hoop petticoat daffodil (Europe)

They have long open tubular flowers, which are usually golden but which can be paler.

N. cyclamineus (Portugal)

An outstanding narcissus with heavily reflexed perianths. Golden yellow flowers on 15 cm stems, which first appear in early September and last for at least four weeks. One of the best. It does increase in our soils and climate.

N. 'Hawera'

A beautiful hybrid with *N. triandrus*. It has soft yellow flowers with slightly reflexed perianths.

N. 'Nylon'

A winter flowering plant with creamy white trumpets derived from *N. bulbocodium*.

Nerine – Spider lily (South Africa)

An excellent autumn flowering bulb which seems to cope with our climate very well.

N. bowdenii

One of the better-known species. The flower scapes are 45 to 60 cm tall, each carrying a number of bright pink blooms.

N. filifolia

A low-growing species 15–25 cm tall with flower scapes carrying a number of small spidery red flowers in summer and autumn.

Nomocharis (Himalaya, West China and Tibet)

This is a wonderful genus of only five species which are allied to *Lilium* and *Fritillaria*. In our garden some success has been achieved over the years but the ideal formula for regular successful flowering has yet to be discovered. A limited supply of bulbs is offered by Southwell Plants and these are probably seedlings of *N. pardanthina,* all very beautiful.

Other species include *N. mairei* (heavily speckled) and *N. saluenensis* (deep rose pink). Like meconopsis they do very well in Scotland, cold comfort to us here. They grow to about 30 cm in height with flowers about 5 cm across, white to pale pink often heavily spotted.

It is difficult to explain why these lily-like plants should be so appealing. They are certainly one of the aristocrats of the plant world and to see one is to want to grow it.

Oenothera – Evening primrose

Useful summer flowering plants.

Nomocharis pardanthina

O. fruticosa
Canary yellow flowers over a long period. 30 cm.

O. missouriensis
Prostrate growth with large yellow flowers over a long period.
30 cm tall x 60 cm wide.

Oxalis (South Africa and tropical America)
This name can send shivers to a lot of gardeners but there are one or
two species which don't get out of control.

O. adenophylla
Funnel-shaped flowers of satiny pink. Dies down in winter.
10–12 cm.

O. lobata
Another small plant with bright green leaves, which die away in
spring to reappear in autumn, with yellow flowers.

Oxypetalum syn. – Tweedia caeruleum (Brazil and Uruguay)

Starry light blue flowers in summer over a long period. Very attractive and easily kept going from seed. 50 cm.

Paeonia

Already mentioned are a few special plants which somehow capture the imagination. I believe that paeonies belong to this category and they should join the small coterie of garden aristocrats for their unmistakable air of quality and class. They can be divided into two classes, or rather three, as the tree paeonies have already been dealt with.

First there are the many beautiful named hybrids with outstanding blends of colours. All of these thrive in our region. They obviously like the cold period of dormancy and hot summers and good drainage. Flowering of paeonies improves as the plant ages and feeding with compost is an aid to this.

As always, the hybrids can be chosen by form and colour. Less easily obtained, but in my view equally desirable, are some of the species

Paeonia 'Buckeye Belle'

Paeonia cambessedesii

which have distinctive and attractive foliage as well as flowers of simple beauty. Unfortunately, paeony nurseries have not bothered too much with the latter, being more concerned perhaps with the cut flower export trade.

Here are four outstanding species, which can be obtained occasionally.

P. cambessedesii (Balearic Islands)
A low growing plant with deeply cup-shaped single flowers of soft rose pink. Very beautiful.

P. mlokosewitschii (often referred to as Molly the Witch) (Caucasus)
Soft green leaves and single cup shaped lemon yellow flowers. 50–60 cm.

P. obovata var. *alba* (Siberia, China)
New leaves of unique purplish grey colour with red stems later changing to soft green. Single, white, cup-shaped flowers with red anthers. In our former garden it produced up to 12 seedlings annually, all eagerly sought after.

Paeonia 'Coral Sunset'

Paeonia obovata var. *alba*

Paeonia tenuifolia

P. tenuifolia

Very fine divided foliage surmounted by several large single blood red flowers with golden anthers.

P. 'Buckeye Belle'

Double flowered hybrid of rich blood red.

P. 'Coral Sunset'

Subtle hues of salmon pink through cream to paler shades.

Papaver

Lower growing forms of *P. orientalis* are available with a variety of colours from pink, red, scarlet and salmon. Flowers 10 cm across. Excellent border plant.

Phlox

The dwarf phlox make an excellent front of border plant as well as good ground cover. Flower colours vary from white through pink to deep rose, soft blue and lavender.

P. adsurgens
Stems up to 20 cm of large white to pink flowers.

P. subulata 'Moss Phlox'
A mat forming phlox with the usual range of colours. There are a number of named varieties, all very good.

P. 'Apollo' Deep lavender. 3 cm.

P. 'Iceberg' Ice Blue Flowers. 3 cm.

P. 'Pink Buttons' Compact bright pink. 3 cm.

P. 'Wagon Wheels' – an old favourite for hanging over walls. Sprays of pink flowers. 10 cm.

Taller growing hybrids and cultivars which are semi evergreen are freely available. They have tall spires of flowers, white pink and red. Very hardy summer-flowering perennials.

Polemonium

A blue flowered perennial with attractive foliage making it a good plant for a border.

P. caeruleum
Deep green fern-like foliage and spikes of violet blue flowers. 60 cm.

Platycodon – Balloon flower

A monotypic genus it resembles a campanula and was previously known as *Campanula grandiflorus*. Violet -blue flowers on a plant which reaches 45–60 cm in height. Double white-flowered form as well as pale pink are sometimes offered.

Primula

Most gardeners know something about primulas but few would realise the extent of this very large family of plants which embraces over 500 species. Our region is not really good primula country because the prime requirement of keeping their roots moist through summer is difficult to achieve. Drying out for even a day can be fatal for some and our ever present atmospheric dryness doesn't help either. Nevertheless, quite a range of primulas, both European and Asiatic, can survive if cool moist shady sites are chosen. In our garden we have had some success with both types. The European primulas come from western Europe, the Balkans, Caucasus and Turkey. They are hardy and include a number of old favourites.

P. auricula (European Alps)
This species has pale leathery leaves and clean yellow flowers. In addition, there are numerous hybrids in a great range of colours some with leaves covered by a fine powdery farina, hence the name Dusty Millers.

P. marginata
A handsome foliage plant with powdered leaves which have sharply toothed white edges and lavender-blue flowers.

P. marginata 'Linda Pope'
A beautiful hybrid with bland flowers of glowing mauve. There are a few other named hybrids such as Drake's form, 'Caerulea' and 'Holden Clough', all very good.

P. minima
This has been in our garden for ten years, proving its ability to cope with the climate and soil. Very small leaves on a plant which slowly increases in breadth to up to 20 cm. Violet-mauve flowers of a good size.

The Asiatic species come from countries such as Kashmir, Bhutan, W.China, Tibet and Japan. The most beautiful of all primulas are in this group but many are quite unsuited to our region. There are a few, however, which can be grown without difficulty so long as they are kept cool and moist.

'Candelabra' primulas
A well-known group of woodland primulas with large clumps of leaves and tall stems surmounted by typical tiers of flowers in a wide range of colours. There are several species in this group, the easiest being *P. heladoxa*, a tall plant with bright yellow flowers.

Primula sikkimensis

P. denticulata

An old favourite which has tight globular pom poms of white or mauve flowers and is relatively easy.

P. sikkimensis

This is a tall-stemmed primula with sweetly scented umbels of primrose yellow flowers and is not difficult.

Many of the Asiatic primulas are not long lived even if conditions are favourable and may survive for only three or four years.

The many double-flowered primroses which are currently popular originated at the Barnhaven Nursery in Oregon and they have been carried on in Britain in recent times. They can be blue, soft yellow and deep red.

The old-fashioned gold-laced polyanthus has made a come back in recent years and is a delight. It has gold edged deep maroon flowers with a large yellow centre but like all the rest it must be kept moist and cool.

Pulmonaria – Lungwort

Low-growing leafy plants, leaves variable and flowers pink to brick red and royal blue.

P. longifolia

Long leaves and rich blue flowers.

P. rubra

Soft hairy green leaves, sometimes spotted white with brick red flowers.

Ranunculus

This genus is well-distributed in temperate regions.

R. gramineus (Southwest Europe)

An easy plant with grass-like leaves and small long-lasting yellow flowers.

R. xarendsii (*R. amplexicaulis* x *R. gramineus*) (Europe)
A lovely long-flowering hybrid with strap-like leaves and sulphur yellow flowers on 20 cm stems.

R. lyallii – Mount Cook lily (New Zealand)
This alpine ranunculus or giant buttercup can be grown to produce flowers in cultivation. Very large rounded leaves 20 cm or more across and flower stems 60–80 cm tall with beautiful single white flowers 4–5 cm across and golden stamens. A cool shaded moist corner is best. Even in nature they are not regular flowerers tending to be biennial so flowering in cultivation is likely to be spasmodic.

R. insignis (New Zealand)
Related to *R. lyallii*, it has bright yellow flowers up to 5 cm across and large fleshy leaves. Requires similar conditions to *R. lyallii*.

There are other small ranunculi but these will be described in the Rock Garden section.

Romneya coulteri – Tree poppy

Monotypic genus, a large and tall perennial which likes sun and good drainage. It has magnificent paeony-like white flowers up to 15 cm across with golden stamens. Cut back near the ground each winter.

Salvia

A genus containing hundreds of species, many of them large-growing and fairly rampant.

S. patens
One of the best of the lower-growing species with tall many flowered spikes of deep blue flowers. There is also a pale blue form 'Cambridge Blue'. 45 cm tall.

Sanguinaria canadensis – Bloodroot

Monotypic genus, nowadays the double-flowered form is the one most commonly seen. It has brilliant white flowers of great purity followed by quite large kidney-shaped leaves up to 7 cm across. The single-flowered form is equally beautiful. Increases in area over time.

Stachys byzantina – Lamb's ear

Grown mainly for its silvery felted and soft downy leaves which look well at the front of a border. Flowers not very attractive.

Thalictrum delavayi

A tall, slender and distinctive plant with small dainty leaves and open sprays of delicate lilac-mauve flowers. There is a double-flowered form as well as a white one. It makes a nice contrast among other border plants and is an attractive cut flower. 1.2 to 1.8 m tall. Occasionally available is *T. kiusianum*, a tiny plant with fluffy mauve pink flowers which spreads a little, but not too much. 10 cm.

Trillium

In recent years these wonderful American woodland plants have burst onto the garden scene in spectacular fashion. There are some species native to Asia but the garden plants we grow narrow down to about ten species from North America all of which are well worth seeking.

Each of the plant's stems terminates in a single tier of three leaves from which emerges a three-petalled flower, hence the name *Trillium*. They flower in the second half of October, require a moist cool site, are not fussy as to soil and are very long lived if properly cared for.

After some years they can be divided without difficulty. In fact it becomes necessary to divide them, once they grow too large for their garden situation but it is a good number of years before this happens. They can be somewhat expensive to buy but because of their long life they are a good investment.

In America, hybrids occur in nature but in horticulture they are virtually absent. However, there is such a good choice from the available species that they are really not needed.

Opposite: *Trillium ovatum*

T. chloropetalum

One of the best known, but not necessarily the best, trillium, it can have white, maroon or sometimes pale yellow flowers.

T. erectum

It has small but quite bold flowers of either rich maroon or white with a dark ovary.

T. grandiflorum

One of the best trilliums, with simple elegant white flowers. The double form Flore Pleno is sought after. There is also a beautiful pink form.

T. hibbersonii

This is a smaller cliff dwelling version of T. ovatum.

T. ovatum

An outstanding trillium which we have grown and enjoyed for 20 years. Quite large flowers of purest creamy white.

T. pusillum var. ozarkanum

A lovely plant with smaller white flowers and habit, very free flowering.

T. rivale

A tiny plant, smaller in all its parts with speckled white or pink flowers.

T. rugelii

Puts on a lesser show because it tends to droop its flowers beneath the leaves but adds variety to the Trillium family.

T. sessile

Plants often incorrectly offered under this name. Red or maroon flowered plants are usually T. chloropetalum, T. sessile is a smaller plant and if a good form has small rich red maroon flowers.

For those readers who may become interested in trilliums, they are comprehensively dealt with in a beautifully illustrated book *Trilliums* by Frederick W. Case Jnr. and Roberta B. Case – Timber Press, Portland, Oregon.

Tulipa

Like other plants already described, these can be divided into two categories. Firstly, there are the flamboyant hybrids much used as bedding plants in public places where they can brighten otherwise sombre areas. They don't blend so easily into a mixed border because of their very bright colours.

There is however a hybrid called 'Maytime' which is very fine and worth seeking out. It has slender and elegant flowers of a deep wine colour. There is also a greenish white form.

The species tulips are more difficult to obtain but they do pop up in garden centres occasionally. They are usually quite small with flowers of softer colours and more delicate form.

T. sprengeri

Stems 30 to 40 cm high surmounted by slender elegant scarlet flowers streaked with soft yellow on the outside.

T. tarda

A small plant with a white flower and yellow centre.

Ground cover

Ground cover is an essential requirement for every garden where it can cover unplanted areas and suppress weeds. There are not a lot of plants which can be trusted to quietly spread over the ground without getting out of control or growing into surrounding plants but there are a few. One of the chief virtues of good ground cover is that it can be easily removed when the time comes to replace it with something of more importance.

Ajuga

Not a distinguished plant but an easy one, which is not too invasive.

A. genevensis

Less spreading than *A. reptans* with flower spikes of gentian blue.

A. reptans

A stoloniferous plant with blue, rose or white flowers but should be kept away from any choice plants.

Arctostaphylos nevadensis (North America)

A stiff prostrate woody plant with small oval leaves and urn shaped flowers of pink and white. An attractive ground cover.

Coprosma 'Taiko' (New Zealand)

Very prostrate ground hugging native with good foliage.

Dryas octopetala – Mountain aven

Attractive flowers stand up on 7 cm stems from ground-hugging foliage. Layers itself.

Lithodora diffusa

Already mentioned under Perennials, it will spread over an area of 60–80 cm. Small deep green leaves and masses of stemless flowers of rich gentian blue.

Pimelea prostrata – New Zealand daphne

Flat growing with grey foliage and white flowers in summer.

Phlox

The dwarf phlox, also mentioned in Perennials makes an excellent weed-suppressing ground cover that will spread over a considerable area. Very colourful and easily removed.

Tiarella cordifolia – Foam flower (North America)

The ground cover 'supreme'. It meets every requirement being very prostrate, is weed-suppressing, easy to plant and remove, attractive spires of foamy off white flowers and good autumn coloured foliage. What a CV! There are several species but *T. cordifolia* is the one to go for.

Climbers

In our harsh sunlight, climbers create a softening effect on buildings, pergolas and pillars and they can also embellish the trunks of trees. They complement the rest of the garden and are an important part of the landscape.

They do involve quite a lot of pruning but this is the price to pay for plants which have a very strong presence. If they are not properly trained they get out of control and can become a problem. The long tendrils of spring growth must be kept in check.

Many are prolific and attractive flowerers, usually at a level above the rest of the garden giving it an added dimension. Probably the most important genus is *Clematis* where there is a wide choice.

Most appreciate some feeding.

Clematis

C. alpina (Europe)
Lovely nodding blue flowers. Looks well on a wall or fence of moderate height. Fertile soil and cool root run.

C. armandii (China)
Glossy dark green leathery leaves and beautiful creamy white flowers about 6 cm across. Best on a sunny warm wall. Evergreen.

C. macropetala (China, Siberia)
A fine species good for a wall or fence. It has violet-blue flowers in November and December which appear to be double due to paler petaloids. Cool root run.

C. montana (Himalaya)
The best-known and easiest of all, it includes a number of named cultivars with flower colours varying from creamy white, soft pink, rose pink and lilac rose. It requires an annual prune, sometimes to stop it collapsing under its own weight. On a fence it

Clematis montana var. rubens

needs to be well supported and tied. Makes a very good sunscreen hanging down from a pergola or verandah.

C. paniculata (New Zealand)

Our most beautiful native clematis needs to be planted in a cool moist position not too close to the base of a tree, preferably an open foliaged one. It can take some time to establish so patience is needed.

There have been some extremely good hybrids produced as a result of crossing *C. paniculata* with *C. marmoraria*, both of them natives. The clean white flowers are outstanding and last for four weeks or more. They must have a cool, shaded, moist site with a tree trunk close by. Tie the clematis to the trunk.

C. tangutica (China and Mongolia)

This has yellow lantern-shaped flowers followed by masses of silky seed heads. It is at its best along a low fence or wall. The best yellow clematis.

In addition to the above species there are many beautiful named hybrids. They have to be pruned in varying ways after flowering and advice needs to be sought. Clematis wilt is a problem which can be fatal and unfortunately there is not much that can be done about it.

Sometimes the plant will break into renewed growth from the base the following season.

Hedera – Ivy

A well-known genus of evergreen climbers which can attach themselves to any sort of wall by their aerial roots.

H. helix – Common ivy
There is a very large number of named cultivars of this species which encompass both large- and small-leaved sorts with foliage colour from grey to shades of green and a lot of variegation.

There are also quite rampant large-leaved varieties which are used as ground cover, often in public places. When purchasing plants it is better to choose on sight as there is such a range of leaf colour and size.

Lonicera – Honeysuckles

Vigorous climbers, which will grow happily in most soils and will tolerate their heads in both sun or part shade. Flowers are sweetly scented.

L. xbrownii 'Dropmore Scarlet'
Tall growing climber producing clusters of bright scarlet tubular flowers through summer.

L. xheckzottii
A more shrubby climber with long tubular fragrant yellow flowers flushed purple through summer.

L. henryi
Vigorous evergreen or semi evergreen with long pointed leaves, dark green above, paler and glossy beneath. Flowers yellow stained red 2 cm long in summer.

L. xtellmanniana
A very good hybrid with flowers 5 cm long, rich coppery yellow flushed red in bud and borne in terminal clusters, December and January. Prefers semi- or even full shade.

Clematis paniculata – our native beauty

Wisteria (Japan and China)

Last but not least, *Wisteria* is probably the most beautiful of all climbers, much loved and grown extensively in our region. There are three principle species in cultivation – *W. floribunda, W. sinensis and W. venusta.* They like sun and prefer moist fertile soil. Over many years we have got away with ordinary soil but have succeeded because of good drainage and not too much drying out.

Getting plants established may take up to two years but when this occurs they can become vigorous. Pruning becomes necessary and this is a skill to be learnt. They are natural twiners and if allowed to have several leaders this habit will develop in an undesirable way.

It is probably best to try and keep to a single leader even if this does prolong the establishment time. I have managed reasonably well with two leaders but a degree of ruthlessness is needed once they get under way. Some pruning can be carried out at the end of the winter and a second pruning in February.

There is a lot to learn about the management of this excellent climber and patience is needed. As growth continues the leader or leaders must be supported by ties to the pergola or more often the facia board of the roof eave. Strangling can occur if tied too tightly or unsuitable ties are used.

W. floribunda (Japan)

There are quite a number of cultivars with flower colours varying from white flushed mauve to pink or deeper mauve. One of the best is *W. multijuga* 'Alba' which has really long racemes of white tinted lilac, 45 to 60 cm long.

W. sinensis (China)

Perhaps the most popular of the blue wisterias. Fragrant mauve or deep lilac flowers with chunky racemes 20 to 30 cm long before the leaves.

W. venusta

It has the largest flowers of the genus. White slightly fragrant racemes – 15 cm long. There is also a cultivar 'Violacea' with violet coloured flowers.

Rock gardens

For those unfamiliar with this type of garden, it is usually an area of 5, 10, 20 or so square metres, raised up and bolstered with well-placed rocks. These hold the soil in place and provide planting sites for alpines, bulbs and other small treasured plants which could be lost in the larger garden and difficult to care for. It is a concentrated form of gardening using small plants which, when the collection is large enough, can provide a flowering season of four to six months.

A rock garden can be labour intensive but if the area is not great it needn't be. The rocks themselves should be placed to make stepping stone access and places for a kneeling pad for weeding.

In my experience any rock garden, no matter how small, can provide more enjoyment per square metre than any other sort of garden.

Design and Construction
To function properly, the rock garden has to be designed by someone who understands the various planting habitats which have to be accommodated. This does not exclude the average gardener but it is important to know the basics.

Choosing a site
Our summer climate can be hot, windy and dry. If there are options a gentle south or east facing slope will be best so long as it can see the sky. Our own rock garden, whilst raised and well constructed is on a flat site and to give it some protection from the sun in summer, a Japanese crabapple *(Malus floribunda)* was planted on the west side. This is carefully pruned to control shade and has proved very satisfactory.

Soil
When construction gets under way soil has to be built up to a depth of around 60 cm or more at the highest point, falling away in an irregular fashion as the placing of rocks dictates.

In our district getting quality soil is difficult and whatever is obtained needs to be enriched organically with good compost. A compromise is to work some good compost into the soil when planting. Good drainage, which is of great importance, should not be a problem with any of our soils.

The rocks

The rocks are a different matter and gone are the days when we could venture into the countryside and help ourselves. They now have to be purchased and care should be taken to select a shape and size which will be compatible with the proposed area.

It is better to have just a few large semi-rounded stones well placed rather than a large number of small ones, which make the rock garden look like a currant pudding. Small rocks are also of little benefit to the plants. The purpose of the rocks is to help retain the soil in the raised areas and create planting sites for those needing their roots protected from the sun.

Placing the rocks through the uneven raised bed of soil is an artistic challenge, which some can cope with and others will not. If one wishes to invest some money in a special garden like this, then a qualified landscaper with rock garden experience makes the whole project more certain and painless.

Watering

Once a garden has been constructed, watering regularly throughout summer must be planned for. Our rock garden gets watered by an installed system but when there is a lot of wind or a drought sets in, the portable rain sprinkler is used. The soft distribution of water from this never causes scouring or over watering and it seems to be a good back up to the less flexible programmed irrigation. The rain sprinkler is controlled by a clockwork manual timer which is quite inexpensive.

What to plant

As much pleasure can be had from growing any of the easy and well known rock garden plants, as the rarities. The main thing is not to let

The author's rock garden.

the garden be overrun by plants which quickly outgrow their space and which would be better in the herbaceous border.

Choice therefore is important and by far the best way is to stock the garden from the alpine and perennial nurseries although the garden centres do occasionally have a few items. Some gardeners will give up on this, as it involves mail ordering. They can't see the plants in advance and are frightened off by the names, a lot of which will be unfamiliar.

However catalogues do give accurate descriptions as to ultimate size, how to grow the plants, details of flowers and colours and so on. One Southland nursery often includes many full colour illustrations which is a great help. And the prices are so reasonable that a gamble is never going to be costly.

Monitoring

In the first year or so on a not ideal site we experienced a percentage of losses until various plants' likes and dislikes were discovered. Some of these were difficult rarities so some loss was to be expected.

New plantings should be closely watched throughout the growing season and if signs of decline appear a prompt move to another position should be made.

Winter dormancy

A good percentage of plants disappear soon after flowering from October onwards and it is important to mark their position to prevent planting over them, or digging them up accidentally. This means inserting a plant label well into the ground beside them. Better still, write the plant name on it with an indelible pen.

Identification

It is surprising how many competent gardeners have great difficulty naming many of the plants in their garden. Remembering any but the common names (where they exist) is not easy and for those who are willing to take the trouble it is at least a good idea to keep all the labels from the plants somewhere where they won't be lost. Better still, area plans of the garden with names recorded in approximate positions give the owner a good control of plant names and satisfaction in knowing what he or she has accumulated in the garden.

Initial planting

To plant out even a small rock garden requires a lot more plants than imagined and it takes two or three years to do the job properly.

It is a mistake to rush at it as too many mistakes will be made. Better to proceed quietly and get a feel for what the garden and environment is capable of. The alternative of using larger plants to cover the ground quickly defeats the purpose and should be resisted.

To create a balanced landscape in the rock garden the highest point may be planted with a taller more dominant shrub such as a slender dwarf conifer with a height not to exceed about 80 cm. This provides a focal point.

Lesser high points can be planted with correspondingly smaller plants. True dwarf rhododendrons are attractive and are evergreen. It is a good idea to have key parts of the garden planted with evergreens so that there is still something there in the off season.

THE PLANTS

The selection below of mostly easy plants follows a rough chronological sequence of flowering. Properly planted, the rock garden can provide interest for much of the year.

Ranunculus calandrinioides
Rarely available, but a gem. A small plant with narrow light grey-green leaves and apple blossom pink flowers for up to 6 weeks in July/August.

Ranunculus ×arendsii
Sold by the nurseries as Ranunculus hybrid it has soft yellow flowers and strap like leaves. Very long flowering – August to October.

Eranthis hyemalis – Winter aconite
Wonderful show of buttercup yellow flowers August/September.

Chionodoxa gigantea – Glory of the snows
Large sky blue flowers with white centres. Flowers for three weeks in September and increases quite rapidly.

Ranunculus calandrinioides

Eranthis hyemalis (Winter aconite)

Fritillaria meleagris
Nodding bells of grey-purple or white. Easy. Flowers September.

Narcissus cyclamineus
A superb early spring bulb. Golden yellow heavily reflexed flowers for at least four weeks (September).

Cyclamen coum
The winter cyclamen. Deep green leaves and soft pink flowers in September.

Pulsatilla vulgaris – Pasque flower
Once included with the anemones, this well known, easy and hardy plant thrives here. It also seeds around a little. White, maroon, purple, mauve and pink. Flowers in October.

Gentiana acaulis – European gentian
Plant only in a moist, fertile site which won't dry out over summer. Brilliant velvety blue trumpets in October.

Narcissus cyclamineus and *Iris reticulata* – harbingers of spring

Pulsatilla vulgaris 'Papageno'

Jeffersonia dubia – a beautiful American woodlander

Ranunculus amplexicaulis

A clean little plant with attractive, blue-green elliptic leaves and white flowers on long stems. Flowers October.

Jeffersonia dubia

A very beautiful plant from Manchuria. The soft lilac flowers on long very thin stems appear before the leaves. It is not difficult but does much better in a moist situation. Flowers October.

Rhododendron

The dwarf rhododendrons enhance a rock garden, in both flower and leaf. They are usually only available from the specialist growers and the alpine and perennial nurseries. Flowers October/November.

Dwarf conifers

There are a few dwarf conifers which look great in this setting and being evergreen help out in the off season. Only available from the alpine and perennial nurseries.

Daphne

There are a number of daphnes which are ideal, but only a few are available.

D. arbuscula

A slow-growing, long-lived compact little bush with violet flowers tinged white. Easy to grow, but hard to obtain.

D. blagayana

Prostrate plant which meanders quietly. Cream scented flowers. Flowers October.

D. cneorum

Eventually becomes a small bush but worth its place. A beautiful scented daphne, which every gardener should have. Flowers October.

Corydalis cashmeriana

Not to be confused with the rampant and invasive C. flexuosa which has electric blue flowers. This is a small gem with flowers of sky blue. Moist site with part shade. Flowers October/November.

Anemonella thalictroides

Don't be put off by the name. This is an easy little plant with the daintiest of leaves and flowers which are white or pale lavender. Flowers November.

Anemone magellanica

A very easy plant with creamy flowers on 35 cm stems. Flowers November.

Aethionema 'Warley Rose'

An absolute first choice for the rock garden. A low growing and speading plant with rich pink flowers over several weeks. Easy. Flowers November.

Androsace sarmentosa

Bright pink flowers on 10 cm stems. Flowers November.

Aster

An excellent plant with purple or violet-purple flowers usually with orange centres. A. alpinus and A. farreri are two worth considering. Flowers November.

Celmisia brevifolia – New Zealand daisy

A small leaved celmisia which has proved to be the easiest to grow and keep for any length of time. The nurseries now offer *Celmisia* hybrids that are very good and much easier than the species. Flowers November.

Penstemon

A wonderful, small group of plants not to be confused with their larger summer-flowering brethren. Flower in November.

P. rupicola
A prostrate plant with deep rose pink tubular flowers in profusion.

P. menziesii
A smaller plant, prostrate with tubular violet mauve flowers.

P. heterophyllus 'True Blue'
A taller plant to 30 cm with lovely sky blue flowers.

P. pinifolius
Needle-like leaves and narrow scarlet trumpet flowers.

Dianthus

The alpine plant nurseries offer a variety of small *Dianthus* hybrids with flowers which are white, bright pink to deep red. All very good.

Aquilegia

There are two very worthwhile species. Both flower in November.

A. bertolonii
A tiny plant with nodding violet blue flowers.

A. canadensis
Small plant with red flowers tipped gold. Attractive.

Hebe buchananii

A very low-growing hebe with tiny leaves. It expands over time to about 50 cm or more. Very compact, native plant.

Helichrysum selago

It doesn't have obvious flowers but is a most attractive whipcord foliage plant. Low growing and spreading to about 40–50 cm.

Penstemon rupicola

Lewisia hybrids

These succulents do well in our region and have stems carrying up to four veined bright pink flowers. For the enthusiast there is a beautiful species *L. tweedyi* which has large soft apricot flowers and handsome leaves.

Heliohebe raoulii

A very tight, prostrate native plant which spreads slowly and fits into the rock garden very well. Mauve flowers in summer.

Lewisia tweedyi

Saxifraga

From flat rosettes of leaves, slender stems carry flowers that can be pink or white. Lovely plants from the European Alps. They like lime. There are many saxifrages with different foliage and flowering habit. All are good, summer-flowering rock garden plants.

Cyclamen hederifolium

A fine autumn-flowering cyclamen with either pink or white flowers. Easy.

Gentiana – Asiatic hybrids

Southwell Plants at Hillend, Balclutha have specialised in these plants recently. Their most popular are:

G. 'Drakes Strain'

A famous hybrid from Scotland, which has large trumpets of Cambridge blue. Moist cool site.

G. 'Southwell Super'

Large rich blue trumpets from the same nursery. Moist cool site.

If any reader has been encouraged to experiment and make a start with this addictive form of gardening, the foregoing list touches only lightly on the possibilities. With interest aroused, the alpine nurseries can satisfy the wishes of the most ardent. For any further inspiration, I highly recommend a spring visit to the rock garden at the Dunedin Botanic Garden. This follows the steep west slope above Lindsay's Creek and is some 150 m long. The many large rocks are expertly positioned in a very natural way creating hundreds of equally natural planting sites for a vast number of plants which are well cared for and clearly labelled. It is probably the best public rock garden in New Zealand and an education to all who visit it.

For my part, I have had a rock garden of one sort or another for forty years. Today, with a little more leisure time, I enjoy this form of gardening more than ever. This is the best testimonial I can offer.

References

Publications

Allan, H.H., *Flora of New Zealand* (Wellington: Government Printer, 1961)

Blue Mountain Nurseries Shrub & Rhododendron Catalogue (Tapanui: Blue Mountain Nurseries, 2003)

Grace, Julie ed., *Ornamental Conifers* (Newton Abbott: David & Charles,1988)

Griffith, Anna N., *Collins Guide to Alpines* (London: Collins, 1964)

Grey-Wilson, Christopher, *A Manual of Alpine and Rock Garden Plants* (Portland: Timber Press, 1989)

Harrison, Richmond, *Trees & Shrubs* (Wellington: A.H. & A.W. Reed, 1981)

Harkness, Bernard E. and Mabel G.Harkness, *Seedlist Handbook* (Portland: Timber Press, 1993)

Manual of Trees & Shrubs, 5th Edn (Romsey: Hillier Nurseries, 1984)

Mark, A.F. and Nancy M. Adams, *New Zealand Alpine Plants* (Auckland: Godwit Press, 1995)

Mathew, Brian, *Hellebores* (Woking: Alpine Garden Society, 1989)

Phillips, Roger and Martyn Rix, *Perennials Vols. 1 & 2*, (London: Pan Books, 1991)

_____ *The Bulb Book* (London: Pan Books, 1981)

Redgrove, Hugh ed., *A New Zealand Handbook of Bulbs & Perennials* (Auckland: Godwit Press, 1991)

Other

MetService Weather Statistics

Plant sources

Southwell Plants, Hillend, No.2 R.D., Balclutha.
Heather and John Metherell. Tel. (03) 418 2465. Fax (03) 418 2475.
Alpines, Perennials, specialists in *Gentiana* and *Primula*.
Mail order only.

Hokonui Alpines, R.D. 6 Gore.
Peter and Louise Salmond. Tel. (03) 208 9609.
Alpines including N.Z. alpines, perennials. Nursery open to the
public as well as mail order. Closed Sundays and public holidays.

Both of the above nurseries offer a comprehensive range of plants through
catalogues, which are posted each spring and autumn to anyone who
wishes to get on their mailing list.

The **Dunedin Rhododendron Group**, P.O.Box 5052, Dunedin. Issues to
members in March/April each year a comprehensive list of *Rhododendron*
species and hybrids, which includes both dwarf species and hybrids. Plants
are couriered to country members. The Group also publishes *The Bulletin*
annually, of some 100 pages. This contains articles on gardens in New
Zealand and overseas as well as much about rhododendrons and all sorts
of other plants. They also arrange garden tours to various parts of the region.
Annual subscription is $22.

Blue Mountain Nurseries, Tapanui.
Tel. (03) 204 8250. Fax (03) 204 8278.
Very wide range of all trees, shrubs, conifers, natives,
Rhododendron specialists.

Ribbonwood Nurseries, Glenelg St., Dunedin.
Tel. (03) 453 4673. Fax (03) 453 4678.
Native plant specialists.

Numbers in bold indicate a
   photograph.

Abelia 'Edward Goucher' 70
Abelia ×grandiflora 70
Abies balsamea 'Nana' 60
Abies koreana 66
Abies nordmanniana 66
Abies pinsapo 66
Abutilon 'Ashford Red' 70, **71**, 71
Abutilon vitifolium 71
Acacia 36
Acer capillipes 36
Acer davidii 36
Acer davidii 'George Forrest' 36
Acer griseum 36
Acer japonicum 'Aconitifolium' 39
Acer negundo 38
Acer palmatum 13, 38
Acer palmatum dissectum 38
Acer palmatum 'Senkaki' 38
Acer platanoides 38
Acer rubrum 24, 38
Aesculus carnea 'Briotii' 55
Aesculus indica **39**, 55
Aesculus pavia 38, **39**
Aethionema 'Warley Rose' 159
Agapanthus orientalis 106
Ajuga genevensis 144
Ajuga reptans 144
Albizzia julibrissin 'Rosea' 39
Alchemilla mollis 107
Alstroemeria 33, 107, **107**
Althaea 108
Amelanchier canadensis 39
Androsace sarmentosa 159
Anemone 33
Anemone blanda 108
Anemone ×fulgens 108
Anemone japonica 108
Anemone magellanica 159
Anemone nemorosa 108
Anemone obtusiloba patula 109
Anemone sylvestris 109
Anemonella thalictroides 159
Aquilegia 33
Aquilegia bertolonii 109, 160
Aquilegia canadensis 109, **109**, 160
Aquilegia flabellata 110
Arctostaphylos nevadensis 33, 144
Armeria maritima 110
ash 42
Astelia 31
Aster alpinus 110, 159
Aster farreri 110, 159
Astilbe 33, 106, 110
atlas cedar 66
Azalea – see Rhododendron 14, 24, 71
Azara microphylla 40

beauty bush 88
beech 31, 56
Betula jacquemontii 56
Betula papyrifera 56
Betula pendula 56
Berberis thunbergii 'Atropurpurea' 72
Berberis thunbergii 'Kobold' 72
Berberis thunbergii 'Gold Rim' 72
Bergenia 110
birch 23, 56
broadleaf 43
broom 78

calico bush 87
Californian lilac 74
Camellia 14, 24, 27, 72
Camellia 'Cornish Snow' 72
Camellia 'Barbara Clark' 74
Camellia 'Donation' 74
Camellia 'Moshio' 73
Camellia 'Quintessence' 73
Camellia reticulata 73
Camellia saluenensis 74
Camellia sasanqua 74
Camellia ×williamsii 74
Campanula 33
Campanula betulaefolia 111
Campanula carpatica 111
Campanula cochlearifolia 111
Campanula garganica 111
Campanula rotundifolia 111
campion 124
candytuft 120
Ceanothus 'Henri Desfosse' 74
Ceanothus papillosus var. roweanus
   75
cedar 66
Cedrus atlantica 66
Cedrus deodara 66
Celmisia brevifolia 160
Cercidiphyllum japonicum 40
Cercis canadensis 'Forest Pansy' 40
Cercis siliquastrum 40
Chaenomeles speciosa 'Apple
   Blossom' 75
Chaenomeles 'Mrs Murphy's Red'
   75
Chaenomeles 'Chocharagaki' 75
Chaenomeles 'Dr Burton' 75
Chamaecyparis lawsoniana 'Blue
   Mountain' 62
Chamaecyparis lawsoniana
   'Elwoodii' 62
Chamaecyparis lawsoniana
   'Grayswood Feather' 62
Chamaecyparis lawsoniana 'Green
   Globe' 60
Chamaecyparis lawsoniana 'Hughes'
   62

Chamaecyparis lawsoniana
   'Imbricata Pendula' 62
Chamaecyparis lawsoniana
   'Pembury Blue' 62
Chamaecyparis lawsoniana 'Silver
   Queen' 62
Chamaecyparis lawsoniana
   'Stewartii' 62
Chamaecyparis obtusa 'Kosteri' 60
Chamaecyparis obtusa 'Nana
   Gracilis' 60
Chamaecyparis pisifera 'Boulevard'
   63
Chamaecyparis 'Filifera Nana' 60
Cheiranthus 111
chestnut 38, **39**, 55
Chilean firebush 41
Chimonanthus praecox 75
Chionochloa 32
Chionodoxa gigantea 112, 155
Chrysanthemum 33
Chrysanthemum mawii 112
Cistus ×aquilari 'Maculatus' 75
Cistus 'Anne Palmer' 75
Cistus monspeliensis 75
Cistus 'Silver Pink' 75
claret ash 42
Clematis alpina 146
Clematis armandii 146
Clematis macropetala 146
Clematis montana 146, **147**
Clematis paniculata 147, **149**
Clematis tangutica 147
copper beech 56
Coprosma 'Black Cloud' 76
Coprosma 'Brunette' 76
Coprosma 'Copperfield' 76
Coprosma 'Greensleaves' 76
Coprosma ×kirkii 'Compacta' 76
Coprosma petriei 76
Coprosma rugosa 76
Coprosma 'Taiko' 144
Cornus 15
Cornus 'Cherokee Chief' 77
Cornus 'Eddie's White Wonder' 40
Cornus florida 40
Cornus florida rubra 76
Cornus kousa chinensis 40
Cornus nuttallii 41, **41**
Corokia cotoneaster 77
Corokia 'Geenty's Ghost' 77
Corokia virgata 'Red Wonder' 77
Corydalis cashmeriana 159
Corylopsis spicata 77
Corylopsis willmottiae 77
Cotinus coggygria 15, 26, 41, **42**
Cotoneaster dammeri 'Royal Beauty'
   77
Cotoneaster horizontalis 78

Cotoneaster salicifolius 78
crabapple 46
Cryptomeria japonica 66
Cryptomeria japonica 'Elegans
    Compacta' 63
Cryptomeria japonica 'Elegans
    Aurea' 63
Cryptomeria 'Vilmoriniana' 61
Cupressus sempervirens 'Gracilis' 63
Cupressus sempervirens 'Swane's
    Gold' 63
Cupressus cashmeriana 63, **64**
Cyclamen coum 156
Cyclamen hederifolium 156
cypress 63
Cytisus ×kewensis 78
Cytisus 'Lilac Time' 78
Cytisus 'Burkwoodii' 78

Daphne arbuscula 158, 159
Daphne blagayana 78, 159
Daphne cneorum 78, 159
Daphne mezereum 78
Daphne odora 78
Daphne retusa 79
dawn redwood 67
Delphinium 106, 112
Deutzia gracilis 79
Deutzia 'Niko' 79
Dianthus 33, 160
Dianthus caryophyllus 112
Diascia 'Ruby Field' 112
Digitalis purpurea 113
Disanthus cercidifolius 79
dog's tooth violet 113
dogwood 40, 76
Douglas fir 69
Dryas octopetala 33, 144
dwarf conifers 158

elm 59
Enkianthus campanulatus 79
Embothrium coccineum 41
Epimedium 33
Epimedium niveum 113
Epimedium ×warleyense 113
Erica 79
Erica carnea 80
Erica cerinthoides 80
Erica ×darleyensis 'Darley Dale' 80
Erica ×darleyensis 'A.T.Johnson' 80
Erica ×darleyensis 'Furzey' 80
Erica ×darleyensis 'Mary Helen' 80
Erica ×darleyensis 'Silver Beads' 80
Erica erigena 'Nana' 80
Erica erigena 'Smokey Mauve' 80
Erica erigena 'W.T.Ratcliff' 80
Eranthis hyemalis 113, 155, **156**
Erythronium dens-canis 113

Erythronium revolutum 113, **114**
Erythronium 'White Beauty' 113
Escallonia 'Apple Blossom' 80
Escallonia ×exoniensis 81
Escallonia macrantha rubra 81
Eucalyptus gunnii 56
Eucalyptus nicholii 56
Eucalyptus niphophila 56
Eucalyptus nitens 56
Eucryphia 15
Eucryphia cordifolia 16, 81
Eucryphia glutinosa 82
Eucryphia lucida 82
Eucryphia ×nymensensis 16, **81**, 82
evening primrose 129
Exochorda racemosa 82

Fagus sylvatica 56
Fagus sylvatica 'Riversii' 56
false cypress 60
fir 60, 66
firethorn 51
flax 93
flowering cherry 27, 50
Fothergilla major 82
foxglove 113
Fraxinus ornus 42
Fraxinus oxycarpa 42
Fritillaria meleagris 156
Fuchsia magellanica 'Mrs.Popple' 82
Fuchsia magellanica var. mollinae 82

Garrya elliptica 42
gentian 26
Gentiana 33
Gentiana acaulis 115, **115**, 156
Gentiana 'Drake's Strain' 116, **116**,
    162
Gentiana 'Southwell Super' 116,
    162
Gentiana saxosa 116
Gentiana septemfida 116
Geranium 33
Geranium dalmaticum 117
Geranium himalayense 117, **117**
Geum chilense 117
Geum coccinea 117
Ginkgo biloba 63
Gladiolus tristis 118
Gleditsia triacanthos 'Elegantissima'
    43
Gleditsia triacanthos 'Sunburst' 43
glory of the snows 112, 155
golden rain tree 44
granny's bonnet 109
grape hyacinth 128
Grevillea 'Mt.Tamboritha' 82, 83
Grevillea victoriae 82, 83
Griselinia littoralis 43

gum 56
Gypsophila paniculata 118
Gypsophila repens 'Rosea' 118

Haberlea ferdinandi-coburgii 118
Hamamelis mollis 83
heath 79
Hebe 31, 83
Hebe annulata 83
Hebe buchananii 31, 83, 160
Hebe cupressoides 83
Hebe hulkeana 31, 83
Hebe macrantha 16, 31, 83, **85**
Hebe ochracea 'James Stirling' 83
Hebe odora 83
Hebe pinguifolia 31, 84
Hebe 'Red Edge' 84
Hedera helix 148
Helichrysum coralloides 84
Helichrysum selago 31, 85, 160
Heliohebe raoulii 161
Helleborus 33, 118
Helleborus 'Moonshine' 119
Helleborus orientalis 119
Helleborus 'White Magic' 119
Heuchera micrantha 'Palace Purple'
    119
Heuchera sanguinea 119
Hibiscus syriacus 85
Himalayan poppy 124, 126
holly 43, 87
hollyhock 108
honeysuckle 90, 148
Hosta 'Halcyon' 119, 120
Hosta sieboldii 'Elegans' 120
Hosta sieboldii 'Alba' 120
Hydrangea 16
Hydrangea macrophylla 'Ayesha' 86
Hydrangea macrophylla 'Blue Wave'
    16, 86, **87**
Hydrangea macrophylla 'Holstein' 86
Hydrangea macrophylla 'Lanarth
    White' 86
Hydrangea macrophylla 'Red Star' 86
Hydrangea villosa 16, 86
Hypericum 'Hidcote Gold' 87

Iberis sempervirens 120
Iberis sempervirens 'Little Gem' 120
Ilex altaclerensis 43
Ilex altaclerensis 'Lawsonii' 43
Ilex aquifolium 43
Ilex crenata 'Helleri' 87
Incarvillea delavayi 'Bees Pink' 120
Iris 33
Iris bucharica 121
Iris cristata 123
Iris histrioides 121
Iris reticulata 121, **122**, **157**

Iris ×*sindpur* 121
ivy 148

japonica 75
Jeffersonia dubia **158**, 158
judas tree 40
Juglans regia 56
Juniperus communis 'Hornibrookii' 61
Juniperus ×*media* 'Gold Coast' 61
Juniperus recurva 'Coxii' 63
Juniperus squamata 'Blue Star' 61

Kalmia latifolia 87, **88**
kanuka 32, 44
Kolkwitzia amabilis 'Pink Cloud' 88
Kolreuteria paniculata 44
kowhai 31, 52
Kunzea ericoides 32, 144

Lady's mantle 107
larch 21, 67
Larix decidua 67
larkspur 112
lavender 16, 88
Lavandula angustifolia 'Blue Mountain' 88
Lavandula ×*intermedia* 89
Lavandula stoechas 89
Lavatera 'Barnsley' 123
Lawson's cypress 62
lemonwood 48
Leptospermum 44, 89, **89**, **90**
Lewisia 161, **161**
lilac 104
Lilium auratum 123
Lilium mackliniae 124, **125**
Lilium regale 123
Lilium speciosum 124
lily 123, 124
Liquidambar styraciflua 44
Liriodendron tulipifera 57
Lithodora diffusa 124, 145
Lonicera ×*brownii* 'Dropmore Scarlet' 148
Lonicera ×*heckzottii* 148
Lonicera henryi 148
Lonicera korolkowii 90
Lonicera nitida 90
Lonicera tellmanniana 148
Lophomyrtus ×*ralphii* 'Kathryn' 90, 91
Lophomyrtus ×*ralphii* 'Variegata' 90, 91
lupin 91
Lupinus 91
Lychnis coronaria 'Alba' 124
Lychnis flos-jovis 124

Magnolia campbellii 45
Magnolia grandiflora 45
Magnolia 'Iolanthe' 46
Magnolia liliiflora 91
Magnolia loebneri 91
Magnolia salicifolia 13, **45**, 46
Magnolia sieboldii 46
Magnolia soulangiana 13, 46
Magnolia stellata 13, 46
Magnolia 'Vulcan' 46
Magnolia wilsonii 46
Malus 24
Malus coronaria 47
Malus floribunda 26, 47, 151
Malus ioensis 'Plena' 47
Malus 'Profusion' 47
manna ash 42
manuka 31, 44
maple 36, 38
Meconopsis betonicifolia 126
Meconopsis grandis 126
Meconopsis integrifolia 126
Meconopsis 'Lingholm' 126, **127**
Meconopsis punicea 126
Meconopsis quintuplinerva 126
Meconopsis ×*sheldonii* 126
Mertensia 128
Metasequoia glyptostroboides 67
michaelmas daisy 110, 159
mock orange 93
Muscari armeniacum 128
Muscari azureum 128
Muscari botryoides 128

Nandina domestica 91
Narcissus bulbocodium 128
Narcissus cyclamineus 128, 156, **157**
Narcissus 'Hawera' 129
Narcissus 'Nylon' 129
Nerine bowdenii 129
Nerine filifolia 129
New Zealand lilac 84
Nomocharis 129, **130**
Nothofagus 31

oak 15, 57
Oenothera fruticosa 129, 130
Oenothera missouriensis 130
Olearia 92
oriental poppy 134
Osmanthus delavayi 92
Oxalis adenophylla 130
Oxalis lobata 130
Oxypetalum 131

Pachystegia insignis 32, 92
Paeonia 14, 33, 106, 131
Paeonia 'Buckeye Belle' **131**, 134

Paeonia cambessidesii 132, **132**
Paeonia 'Coral Sunset' **133**, 134
Paeonia delavayi 92
Paeonia lutea 'Ludlowii' 92
Paeonia mlokosewitschii 132
Paeonia obovata var. *alba* 132, **133**
Paeonia suffruticosa 93
Paeonia tenuifolia 134, **134**
Papaver 93
Parrotia persica 47
peach 51
pearl bush 82
Penstemon 16, 33
Penstemon heterophyllus 'True Blue' 160
Penstemon menziesii 160
Penstemon pinifolius 160
Penstemon rupicola 160, **161**
Philadelphus 'Beauclerk' 93
Philadelphus 'Frosty Morn-Bride's Blossom' 93
Philadelphus 'Manteau d'Hermine' 93
Philadelphus 'Virginal-Bride's Blossom' 93
Phlox 33, 134
Phlox adsurgens 135
Phlox 'Apollo' 135
Phlox 'Iceberg' 135
Phlox 'Pink Buttons' 135
Phlox subulata 135
Phlox 'Wagon Wheels' 135
Phormium tenax 93
Photinia ×*fraseri* 'Red Robin' 94
Photinia ×*fraseri* 'Robusta' 94
Picea glauca 'Conica' 61
Picea jezoensis var. *hondoensis* 67
Picea omorika 67, **68**
Picea orientalis 67
Picea pungens 'Koster' 65
Picea smithiana 65
Pieris forrestii 'Wakehurst' 94
Pieris japonica 94
Pimelea prostrata 145
pine 67
Pinus coulteri 67
Pinus patula 67
Pinus sylvestris 69
Pistacia chinensis 48, **49**
Pittosporum eugenioides 32, 48
Pittosporum tenuifolium 32, 48
Pittosporum tenuifolium 'Stephens Island' 32, 48
Platycodon 106, 135
plum 51
Poa 32
Polomonium caeruleum 135
Portugal laurel 51
Potentilla dahurica 'Manchu' 94

Potentilla fruticosa 94
Primula 33, 135
Primula auricula 136
Primula candelabra 136
Primula denticulata 138
Primula heladoxa 136
Primula marginata 136
Primula marginata 'Linda Pope' 136
Primula minima 136
Primula sikkimensis **137**, 138
Prunus 'Accolade' 50
Prunus amanogawa 50
Prunus armeniaca 50
Prunus blireana 51
Prunus cerasifera 'Nigra' 51
Prunus incisa 50
Prunus lusitanica 51
Prunus persica 'Clara Meyer' 51
Prunus sargentii 50
Prunus shirotae 50
Prunus subhirtella 'Autumnalis' 50
Prunus yedoensis 51
Pseudotsuga menziesii 69
Pulmonaria longifolia 138
Pulmonaria rubra 138
Pulsatilla vulgaris 33, 156, **157**
Pyracantha coccinea 51
Pyracantha 'Shawnee' 52

Quercus canariensis xrobur 57
Quercus coccinea 15, 57
Quercus palustris 15, 57, **58**
Quercus robur 15, 57
Quercus rubra 57

Ranunculus 33
Ranunculus amplexicaulis 158
Ranunculus xarendsii 139, 155
Ranunculus calandrinioides 155, **155**
Ranunculus gramineus 138
Ranunculus insignis 139
Ranunculus lyallii 139
Rhododendron 27, 95, 158
Rhododendron augustinii 14, 97
Rhododendron campylogynum 14, **95**, 97
Rhododendron 'Crest' **96**, 99
Rhododendron davidsonianum 97, **97**
Rhododendron hippophaeoides 97
Rhododendron nakaharae 98
Rhododendron occidentale 98, **98**
Rhododendron pogonanthum section 14
Rhododendron radicans 98
Rhododendron 'Scarlet King Kaka' 99, **99**
Rhododendron schlippenbachii 98

Rhododendron yakushimanum 98
Robinia pseudacacia 57
Romneya coulteri 139
Rosa banksiae 'Lutea' 100
Rosa 'Bantry Bay' 100
Rosa 'Bloomfield's Courage' 100
Rosa 'Claire Matin' 100
Rosa 'Complicata' 100
Rosa 'Constance Spry' 101
Rosa 'Double Delight' 101
Rosa 'Dublin Bay' 101
Rosa 'Dupontii' 101
Rosa 'Golden Wings' 101
Rosa 'Iceberg' 101
Rosa 'Margaret Merrill' 101
Rosa 'Meg' 101, **102**
Rosa 'Mutabilis' 101
Rosa 'Nancy Hayward' 101, **102**
Rosa 'Sally Holmes' **103**, 104
Rosa 'Seagull' 104
Rosa 'Sparrieshoop' **103**, 104
rose 14, 99
rosemary 104
Rosmarinus 'Benenden Blue' 104
Rosmarinus 'Lady in White' 104
Rosmarinus 'Lockwood de Forest' 104
Rosmarinus 'Tuscan Blue' 104
rowan 52

Salix babylonica 57
Salvia patens 139
Sanguinaria canadensis 139
Saxifraga 162
Sequoiadendron giganteum 69
smokebush 41
Sophora microphylla 52
Sophora tetraptera 52
Sorbus aria 52
Sorbus aucuparia 52
Sorbus cashmiriana 54
Sorbus hupehensis **53**, 54
spider lily 129
spruce 61, 65, 67
Stachys byzantina 140
Stewartia pseudocamellia 54
Stewartia sinensis 54
Styrax japonica 54
sweet gum 44
Syringa laciniata 104
Syringa microphylla × persica 105
Syringa microphylla 'Superba' 104

Thalictrum delavayi 106, 140
Thuja koraiensis 65
Thuja occidentalis 'Blackman's Blue' 62

Thuja occidentalis 'Caespitosa' 62
Thuja occidentalis 'Fastigiata' 65
Thuja occidentalis 'Holmstrup' 65
Thuja occidentalis 'Pyramidalis' 65
Thuja occidentalis 'Smaragd' 65
Thuja plicata 69
Thujopsis dolobrata 'Nana' 62
Tiarella cordifolia 33, 145
Tilia xeuropea 59
Tilia mongolica 59
Tilia platyphyllos 59
Trillium 16, 140
Trillium chloropetalum 142
Trillium erectum 142
Trillium grandiflorum 142
Trillium hibbersonii 142
Trillium ovatum **141**, 142
Trillium pusillum var. ozarkanum 142
Trillium rivale 142
Trillium rugelii 142
Trillium sessile 142
Tsuga heterophylla 69
tulip 143
tulip tree 57
Tulipa sprengeri 143
Tulipa tarda 143

Ulmus procera 'Louis van Houtte' 59

vanilla tree 40
Viburnum 16
Viburnum xburkwoodii 105
Viburnum carlesii 17, 105
Viburnum plicatum 'Mariesii' 16, 105
Viburnum tinus 'Laurustinus' 105

wallflower 111
walnut 56
Weigela florida 105
Weigela praecox 105
Wellingtonia 69
western hemlock
western red cedar 69
willow 57
winter aconite 113
winter rose 118
winter sweet 75
Wisteria floribunda 150
Wisteria sinensis 150
Wisteria venusta 150
witch hazel 83

Zelkova serrata 59